# The Sock Knitter's HANDBOOK

Expert Advice, Tips, & Tricks

CHARLENE SCHURCH & BETH PARROTT

*Martingale*®
& C O M P A N Y

The Sock Knitter's Handbook: Expert Advice, Tips, and Tricks
© 2012 by Charlene Schurch and Beth Parrott

Martingale & Company
19021 120th Ave. NE, Ste. 102
Bothell, WA 98011-9511 USA
www.martingale-pub.com

Printed in China
17 16 15 14 13 12      8 7 6 5 4 3 2 1

**Library of Congress Cataloging-in-Publication Data
is available upon request.**

ISBN: 978-1-60468-046-1

## MISSION STATEMENT
Dedicated to providing quality products
and service to inspire creativity.

## Credits
President & CEO: Tom Wierzbicki
Editor in Chief: Mary V. Green
Design Director: Paula Schlosser
Managing Editor: Karen Costello Soltys
Technical Editor: Ursula Reikes
Copy Editor: Melissa Bryan
Production Manager: Regina Girard
Cover & Text Designer: Adrienne Smitke
Illustrator: Robin Strobel
Photographer: Brent Kane

# Contents

# Introduction

"All things are difficult until they are easy." This describes how sock knitting often works out for knitters. It's the idea of following instructions without a clear idea of what you're doing or why that makes some knitters fearful of tackling that first pair of socks. Although sock knitting may appear difficult, knitting socks is really just about putting together a series of several different knitting techniques—knitting in the round, turning a heel by knitting back and forth, picking up stitches for a gusset, or shaping a toe. These techniques might strike you as challenging, or perhaps merely interesting. But we see knitting socks as offering an opportunity to do something new and different each time you pick up your needles. With so many options, there's absolutely no reason you need to knit socks the same way over and over again.

The humble sock—knitting that we all gladly walk on—offers rich diversity in technique. This little carry-along volume is designed to be a handbook for sock knitters. It offers instructions and alternatives for knitting socks, including casting on and binding off, working heel variations, and knitting toe alternatives. Plus, our stitch dictionary gives you lots of options for decorating your socks.

We've included information about making your hand-knit socks more durable, sizing socks based on shoe size, and which pattern repeats work with the number of stitches required for a sock. In addition, you'll find hints and tips to make your sock knitting easier and more enjoyable. We worked to have all the information you need to knit socks in one place.

We hope you'll carry this little book with you and refer to it any time you're knitting socks, regardless of the sock pattern you're following. Whether you have questions about fit, or working a heel turn, or the best bind off to do for toe-up socks, you'll find the guidance you need here.

# Sock Architecture

Fundamentally, a sock is a tube of knitting that has one open, stretchy end to let the whole foot enter, a sharp turn for the heel, and then a closed end to fit the toe smoothly. You can start knitting this structure at the top, at the toe,

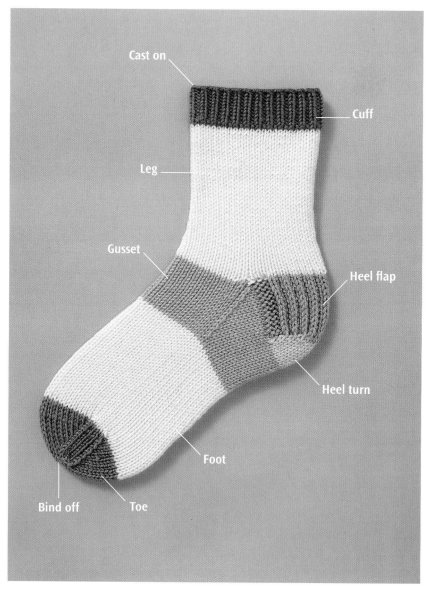

Cast on

Cuff

Leg

Gusset

Heel flap

Heel turn

Foot

Bind off

Toe

Top-down sock

or somewhere in between, such as at the ankle just before the heel. Knitters have been exploring these alternatives forever and no doubt will continue to do so as long as knitting is the best way to make a sock. In this section we describe the individual sock elements and some important fit and wear issues for each one. These examples, one top down and one toe up, have the same elements. Some sock architectures combine or omit an element or two.

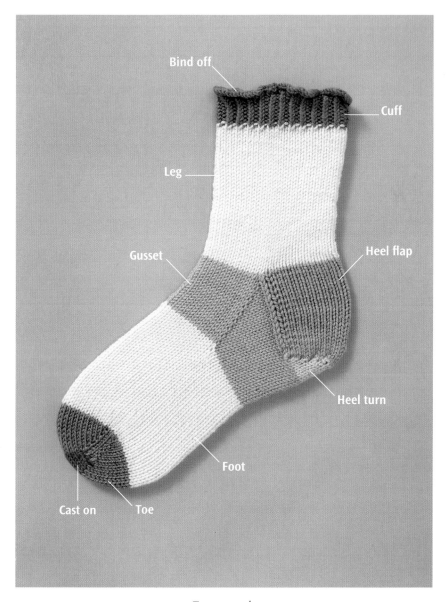

Toe-up sock

## CUFF

The cuff is typically stretchy enough to hold the sock on the calf; it's often worked in ribbing (alternate knits and purls) for elasticity. The top edge of the cuff needs to be loose enough to allow the heel to fit through it. So, if knitting from the top down, the cast-on edge needs to be done loosely using any of the cast ons on page 30. If working from the toe up, the bound-off edge will need to be as elastic as the cuff (page 42).

## LEG

The leg is generally a straight tube that is also elastic enough to accommodate the difference in the circumference between the calf and the ankle. Some knitters like to add shaping to this section around a calf. If you have a ribbed pattern, one way of doing this is to plan how many stitches you need for the difference between the ankle and the calf. Edit the pattern to add those stitches in the purl area of the ribbed pattern. As you work the leg, decrease in the purl part of the pattern. This way the pattern will fit your leg and will look the same for the whole sock. Stretchy ribbed patterns work well for the leg, but this is also the area where some knitters do dazzling pattern work.

## HEEL

The heel is where the tube makes the turn. At its most basic, the heel requires more fabric on the heel side than on the instep side. There are a large number of heel structures to accomplish this. Following is a brief description; instructions for working the individual heel types begin on page 51.

### Short-Row Heels

Short-row heels are worked without changing the number of stitches held on the needles. The knitting takes place on the heel or bottom of the sock, providing the turn required and extra fabric to cover the heel and make a comfortable sock. These socks fit someone with a normal or low instep better than one with a high instep.

### Afterthought, Peasant, or Forethought Heels

These heels are worked as a standard toe; starting with stitches from the leg and foot and working out to the edge of the heel, and then grafting the final stitches together. This is a way to knit all your yarn for the sock and be sure you have enough yarn for the toe, and work the heel in contrasting yarn. Or it's a way to make a bulls-eye heel with self-striping yarn, or to maintain the patterning of self-striping yarn on the leg and foot of a sock. There is no additional fabric for the instep so this sock is best for feet with lower insteps.

## French, Dutch, and Shaped Common Heels

These heels all start with a heel flap that's worked back and forth, allowing the knitter to add reinforcing thread, work a denser knitting pattern (a heel stitch), or use a smaller needle to add durability. Most of these heels have a heel turn (page 52), and then stitches are picked up on the sides of the heel flap. When knitting in the round is resumed, there are more stitches on the needles than there were originally. A gusset is worked decreasing the stitches back to the original number at the beginning of the heel. The length and width of the heel flap and the decrease sequence allows the knitter a lot of flexibility for shape and fit for the foot.

## Strong Heel

As sock knitting evolves, knitters continue to create new ways to turn the tube that we call the sock. The Strong heel (named for Gerdine Crawford-Strong, and described further on page 58) is knit at the same time as the gusset, finishing with a heel turn, making it one of the simplest heel forms to knit.

### New Heel Architecture

Currently a number of knitters are creating new and interesting architectures to knit socks. Some knitters are moving gusset decreases from the side of the foot to the instep or sole, creating new lines and interesting structures for socks. Still others are doing brilliant and interesting sock designs with texture and color.

## FOOT

The foot section is a straight tube between the heel and toe. Many times it's knit in stockinette stitch for speed or ease because it's hidden in the shoe. You can also knit the instep of the foot using the same decorative pattern you used to knit the leg. For those with a narrow foot, an elastic instep pattern such as a rib will help the sock fit comfortably.

## TOE

Not all feet are created equal. Some of us have long toes, some short; some have rather square toes, and some quite pointy. This is one area where you can customize your socks to fit the toes you have. The choice of toe can be based on technique, the length of the toe, or the look. Instructions for individual top-down toes begin on page 74 and toe-up toes start on page 77.

# 🧶 Materials

Basically, all you need are yarn and needles. When it comes to socks, you'll be working in the round, so you'll need either double-pointed needles or circular needles. Let's examine each of these elements a little more closely.

## YARN

Choosing yarn for socks involves selecting the grist; that is, the fiber of the yarn, and the additives to the yarn. Options for grist range from fingering to bulky, depending on the weight of the sock you wish to knit and what kind of shoes or boots you want to wear with the socks. Heavier socks tend to be a good choice when warmth is a priority.

The decision of fiber or blend of fibers is one based on durability, luxury, absorbency, and elasticity. Most sock yarn sold in the United States has a wool component. It's a wonderfully warm, resilient, absorbent fiber, with a natural elasticity that is very comfortable to knit with. The downside of using wool for socks is that it can felt when washed. Many yarns are now labeled "superwash," which means the yarn has been through a process to seal the scales of the wool so that it will not felt. Some yarns have nylon included, which keeps the yarn from shrinking.

Luxury fibers, such as alpaca and silk, are sometimes not as durable as wool. Blending more delicate fiber with wool will extend the wearability of the sock while retaining the desired softness.

If you have wear issues, consider woolly nylon, available at larger sewing stores, to carry along with your sock yarn as you knit areas of the sock that tend to wear out (heels and toes). Some European sock yarns are packaged with a small bobbin of reinforcing yarn to assist with knitting those areas that tend to wear. If your yarn does not come with that option, you might be able to locate the reinforcing yarn you need sold separately, depending on the brand.

It seems to be a current fashion to blend extra fibers with sock yarn. These additives include cotton, bamboo, seacell, and polyamide, but there are a host of others. Some are billed as "green" additives, when in fact we suspect this is a way of selling and marketing what would otherwise be a waste product. Some of these additives may affect the wearability or shrinkage rate of the yarn, and in many cases the fibers are more expensive than wool sock yarn. (We are fundamentally fans of wool sock yarn.)

## Yarn Weights and Suggested Gauges

On many yarns, the ball band gives a suggested needle size and target gauge. In our opinion, this gauge is often too loose for socks, meaning there will be some drape to the fabric. Now, "drape" is a lovely quality for some garments, but not for socks; you want your sock fabric to be firm and dense.

The advantage to knitting a tighter fabric for socks is that the fabric is more durable, which is important if you don't want to reknit or learn how to darn socks. It also makes the socks more comfortable. If the stitches are looser, they tend to dig into the bottom of your foot. When you knit more tightly, a more uniform surface touches the foot. The disadvantage of thicker fabric is that it takes more yarn. This may require you to purchase an extra ball of yarn for a large foot.

The following table lists four yarn weights with the recommended stitches over 1" of knitting and the suggested needle sizes for socks. Note that the gauge and needle sizes for socks is different from the standard sizes for sweaters knit from the same yarns.

| Suggested Gauge and Needle Size | | |
|---|---|---|
| YARN WEIGHT | STITCH GAUGE PER INCH | NEEDLE SIZE |
| Fingering | 8½ to 10 sts | U.S. 0 (2.0 mm) or 1 (2.25 mm) |
| Sport | 7½ to 9 sts | U.S. 2 (2.5 mm) |
| DK | 6½ to 8 sts | U.S. 3 (3.25 mm) |
| Worsted | 6 to 7 sts | U.S. 4 (3.5 mm) |

The following table indicates the approximate number of yards you can expect to find in 50-gram and 100-gram skeins or balls of yarn.

| Yardage Yields | | |
|---|---|---|
| YARN WEIGHT | YARDS PER 50 G | YARDS PER 100 G |
| Fingering | 180 to 230 | 360 to 460 |
| Sport | 150 to 180 | 300 to 360 |
| DK | 120 to 145 | 240 to 290 |
| Worsted | 100 to 110 | 200 to 220 |

# How Much Yarn Does It Take to Knit a Pair of Socks?

The answer to this common question depends—on the weight of the yarn, the size needles you're using, the size of the foot you're knitting for, the texture pattern chosen (for example, cables take more yarn), and the density of the fabric you're creating.

Below is a chart of approximate yardage for socks knit with a single yarn. We've found that stranded knitting, as in Fair Isle patterning, can take up to 25% more yarn than knitting the same fabric with one yarn. Mosaic, slipped-stitch patterning is also denser than plain knitting, so you should consider buying more yarn when working these patterns. With experience, you'll begin to know how much yarn to buy. We suggest buying one ball more than you think you'll need; many yarn shops will take it back in trade, and you'll avoid anxious hours wondering if you have enough.

## Approximate Yards Needed for a Pair of Socks

| YARN WEIGHT | CHILDREN (SMALL) | CHILDREN (MEDIUM) | WOMEN | MEN |
|---|---|---|---|---|
| Fingering | 275 | 340 | 430 | 525 |
| Sport | 215 | 275 | 370 | 430 |
| DK | 200 | 250 | 340 | 400 |
| Worsted | 185 | 215 | 310 | 370 |

## NEEDLES

Socks were historically knit with double-pointed needles. Recently, however, knitters have started using circular needles. Some knitters have difficulty with laddering (the looseness of the stitches between double-pointed needles and the float between stitches that looks like a ladder in the middle of the dense sock fabric), and they find that working with a circular needle lessens this tendency. While figuring out which approach is right for you, there are some other decisions about needles that are important as well. The length of the business end of the needle (the needle part of the circular needle or the length of a double-pointed needle) affects your comfort when knitting. Before you purchase needles, see if you can test them at a shop or borrow some from a friend to try. If that's not possible, at least try one pair or set before you buy a whole set of every size.

## Needle Material

Both double-pointed and circular needles are available in metal (steel, nickel, and aluminum), wood, bamboo, plastic, nylon, casein, and carbon fiber. The difference in material affects the weight of the needles as well as their warmth in your hand. Some needles are more flexible than others. It's important to know if your hands prefer holding rigid needles or ones that offer some give. Some bamboo or laminated wood needles may wear or split if you're a firm knitter, or the friction of knitting with wooden needles may result in a smaller needle size over time.

## Needle Points

The points of knitting needles range from long and slender to short and stubby. Many sock knitters opt for the longer points, as they make decreasing and working texture patterns simpler. Be aware that if you're using yarn that splits, the long, slender points will increase the likelihood of splitting more than with a stubbier needle.

## Length of Double-Pointed Needles

Double-pointed needles are available in lengths from 4" to more than 12". You should base your choice on the size of your hands, the size of the item you're making, and how you hold the needles while knitting. Very short needles may be perfect for a child's sock, but not long enough for an adult sock. Conversely, overly long double points may be unwieldy when knitting a sock.

## Circular Needles

A circular needle consists of two rigid needle sections attached by a cable. The important items to think about when selecting a circular needle are the length of the needle section, the join of the needle to the cable (if it's not smooth, you may have many frustrating hours slipping stitches along this uneven join), and the material the needle is made of (see "Needle Material" above). The flexibility of the cable is also important; it should be soft and pliable, not stiff.

#  Gauge

The knitting gauge is equal to the number of stitches and rows or rounds in an inch. It's important to knit a test swatch and then measure the number of stitches in an inch to see how your swatch compares to the gauge in the pattern. This will let you know if you're knitting at the same density as the pattern designer intended. Using foot circumference and stitch gauge, you'll know how many stitches your sock needs.

The gauge and density of the knitted fabric are directly related to the durability of the socks. Some sock yarns give a recommended needle size and gauge that is looser than optimum for good sock durability. The knitted fabric shouldn't be see-through or have a drape. While those characteristics are good for a sweater, this fabric will be abraded between your foot and shoe or your foot and the floor. It's much simpler to knit dense socks than to knit them loosely and have to fix them later.

## STITCH GAUGE

The ideal is to knit a gauge swatch in the round with the sock pattern you're using, and measure the gauge of your decorative pattern along with the stockinette stitch. It's important to know the true gauge when working patterns that have many slipped stitches (making a denser fabric) or are quite lacy (yielding a looser fabric), as both of these may greatly affect your gauge.

For a simple ribbed pattern you may work a flat stockinette gauge swatch. It will give you almost as much information as a circular one will and you're more likely to work this gauge swatch as the one in the round. One way to keep track of which size needles you've used is to work a number of holes in the fabric that correspond to the needle size. For instance, with a size 2 needle, make two holes by working (YO, K2tog) twice. As you knit you'll see the two little holes and know which size needles you were using.

If you're working with several needle sizes, it's handy to make a row that separates the two or more gauge samples. Some people just knit a reverse stockinette row. This will show you the difference, but you do not know how many rows the previous needle size affects the next gauge sample on different needles. Another alternative is to work one row K1, *(YO, K1), repeat from * to end of row. This doubles the number of stitches on the needle. On the next row: P1, *drop YO, P1, repeat from * to end of row. After you drop the yarn overs, you're back to the original number of stitches. What you'll see once you've knit the next gauge sample is a line of very long stitches—this separates the tension from one needle size to the other.

## THE IMPORTANCE OF ROW GAUGE

Some heel forms, such as the French, short row, Strong, and shaped common, rely on a formula for the length of the heel based on the number of stitches in the sock. Many of the toe instructions also rely on this "standard" proportion. If your row gauge is not standard, you may end up with heels and toes that do not fit as well as you had hoped. We like to use the proportion of 70%, which means that for 10 rows or rounds of knitting to the inch, the stitch gauge will be seven stitches to the inch.

If you have a good idea of the number of stitches you'll need for your sock, cast on and knit your ribbing for an inch. Count the stitches to determine your row gauge, multiply this number by 70% (x 0.7), and you have your stitch gauge. This allows you to check that the sock yarn and needles you're using are on gauge without a large investment of knitting—and if you're on the right track, you can continue with the rest of the sock. If you need to adjust the number of stitches by just a few (10% or fewer), increase or decrease in the last row of the cuff. If your sock needs more than a 10% adjustment in stitches, it's best to cast on and start over.

## NEGATIVE EASE AND GAUGE

Some sock knitters like their socks to have a very snug fit. They'll measure their foot and take a gauge and then subtract 5% to 10% or more as negative ease for sock knitting. The socks that they knit typically have a stockinette foot. We haven't included any negative ease in the "Foot Measurements and Shoe Sizes Chart" on page 123. We've found that when using a ribbed pattern on the leg and instep, any excess fabric is taken up in the elasticity of the pattern and the knitting.

You should keep a few words of caution in mind if using negative ease. When knitting the foot of the sock, make sure it fits; stretching the fabric will make it shorter. If you're knitting only from measuring for the length and have a lot of negative ease, the sock may not be long enough. It may be best to try on a sock before knitting the toe (top down) or heel (toe up) to make sure the foot is long enough. Additionally, fibers that are under tension—really stretched on the foot—will wear out faster than socks that are less stretched on the foot.

If you want to use negative ease, multiply the circumference of the foot times your stitch gauge, subtract the amount of negative ease, and use the resulting number in the patterns. For example, if your foot measures 7", your stitch gauge is 6 stitches per inch, and you want 5% negative ease, you'll want to cast on 40 stitches for your sock: 7 x 6 = 42 - 2 (5%) = 40 stitches.

# Sock Construction

Designing a sock involves a series of decisions about the individual parts of the sock. Many knitters select a sock pattern based solely on the decorative stitch pattern. While this is an important consideration, stopping there may mean losing out on many options that will give you a more satisfying knitting experience, not to mention better-fitting or longer-wearing socks. In this section we'll present some of those easily overlooked options. When you knit your next pair of socks, you may want to substitute one or more parts to make the socks fit better, wear longer, or simply provide an interesting new knitting adventure.

One of the fundamental decisions is whether to begin at the cuff or the toe—working top down or toe up. People give many different reasons for their choice, including fit, fear of running out of yarn before the toe is complete, or avoidance of a technique such as grafting the toe stitches with Kitchener stitch. We'll review the options here, and then in "Knitting Techniques" beginning on page 30, we'll explain how these various approaches work so that you can knit in the direction you choose and incorporate the elements that you like.

## TOP-DOWN SOCKS

Here are five socks knit with the same number of stitches and the same number of rounds in the leg as well as the foot. The leg and foot are knit in white/cream to show that this would be the place for you to pick a decorative pattern or use fancy hand-painted yarn. The cast on is in orange, the cuff is in purple, the heel flap in green, the heel turn in yellow, the gusset in pink, and the toe in teal. Let's explore the elements individually.

Sock A

*Long-tail cast on; K1, P1 rib cuff; French heel; standard round toe*

*Sideways garter cuff;*
*French heel; short-row toe*

*Hemmed cuff with provisional cast on;*
*Dutch heel; 6-gored toe*

*Picot cast on; eccentric rib cuff; shaped*
*common heel; standard pointy toe*

*Long-tail cast on; K3, P3 rib cuff;*
*Strong heel; mitten toe*

## Cast Ons and Cuffs

It's important to cast on loosely enough so that the ribbing, not the cast on, is holding up the sock. The cuff holds the sock on the leg. Most cuffs are worked in some kind of ribbing to make them stretchy and to fit well. Beyond function we have included some decorative cast ons and cuffs. Most cast ons and most cuffs can be worked for top-down or toe-up socks. Techniques for cast ons begin on page 30 and cuffs begin on page 42.

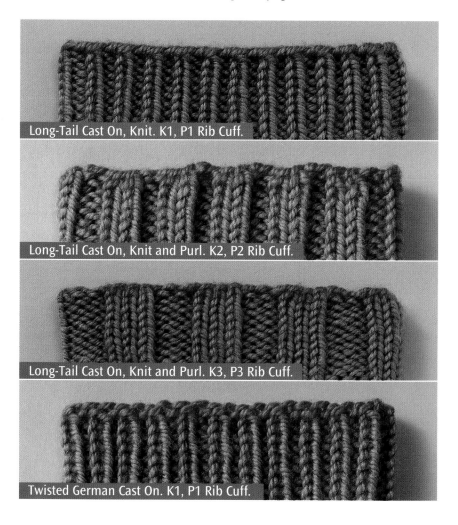

Long-Tail Cast On, Knit. K1, P1 Rib Cuff.

Long-Tail Cast On, Knit and Purl. K2, P2 Rib Cuff.

Long-Tail Cast On, Knit and Purl. K3, P3 Rib Cuff.

Twisted German Cast On. K1, P1 Rib Cuff.

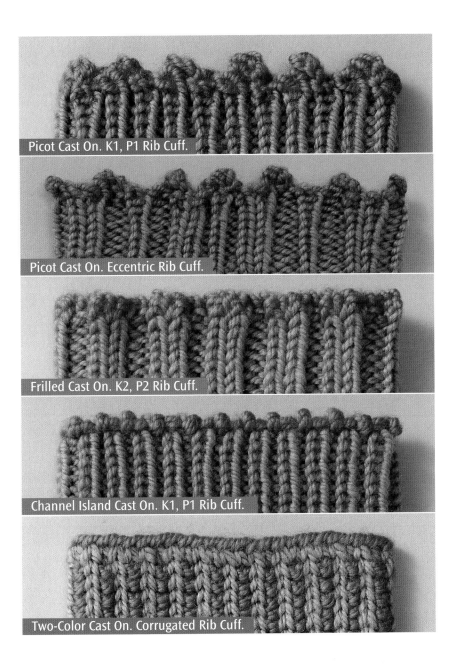

Picot Cast On. K1, P1 Rib Cuff.

Picot Cast On. Eccentric Rib Cuff.

Frilled Cast On. K2, P2 Rib Cuff.

Channel Island Cast On. K1, P1 Rib Cuff.

Two-Color Cast On. Corrugated Rib Cuff.

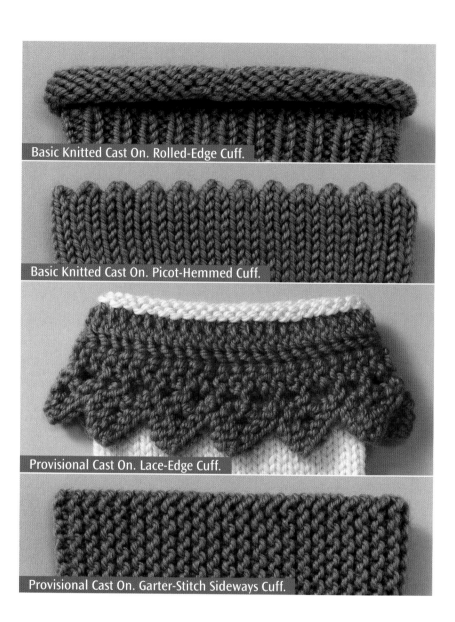

Basic Knitted Cast On. Rolled-Edge Cuff.

Basic Knitted Cast On. Picot-Hemmed Cuff.

Provisional Cast On. Lace-Edge Cuff.

Provisional Cast On. Garter-Stitch Sideways Cuff.

## Foot

The "foot" of a sock is the portion between the heel and the toe. The foot of the sock is a tube, typically worked in the same number of stitches as the leg. It can be knit in stockinette stitch or with the patterning from the leg continued on the instep.

## Heels

Once you've decided to knit a top-down sock, the most important decision is the type of heel to knit. Many knitters select a heel based on ease of working it, but looking at the sock architecture, the heel selection may affect the fit of the sock. The heel portion of the sample socks is knit in green, yellow, and pink. Instructions for heels begin on page 51.

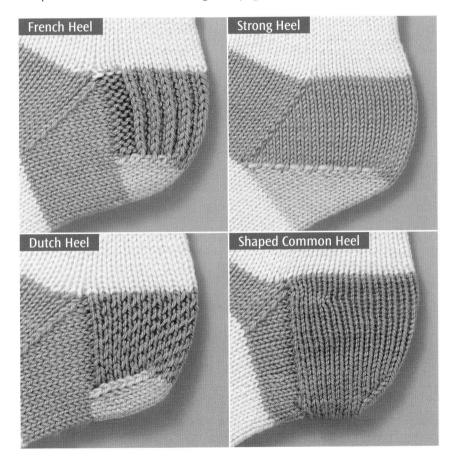

Here are four types of heels, viewed from the bottom. The French heel has a little trapezoid, and the Dutch heel has a small square heel turn. All have generous gussets, providing room for a higher instep. The Strong heel has the largest heel turn. The shaped common heel is worked without a heel turn and has a smaller gusset. For the Strong heel, the length of the heel and gusset are worked together with a larger heel turn, making for simpler knitting.

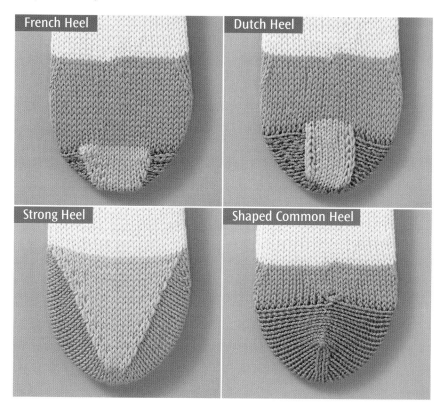

## Toes

Not all feet are created equal. Some of us have long toes, some short, some have rather square toes, and some quite pointy. This is one area where you can customize your socks to fit the toes you have. Some people with pointy toes like to knit asymmetrical socks to fit the foot exactly. While this may seem like a good idea to have a right and left sock, you'll be wearing the sock on the same foot all the time, which means wear will always occur in the same places. Perhaps randomly wearing left and right socks will wear slightly differently, yielding longer-lasting socks.

Choosing a type of toe can be based on technique; there are several that do not required Kitchener grafting. Length of toes is also an important consideration. The standard toe can be worked to be long, whereas the gored toe and short-row toe will be shorter. Choose the option that makes the most sense for the length of the wearer's toes. Instructions for top-down toes begin on page 74.

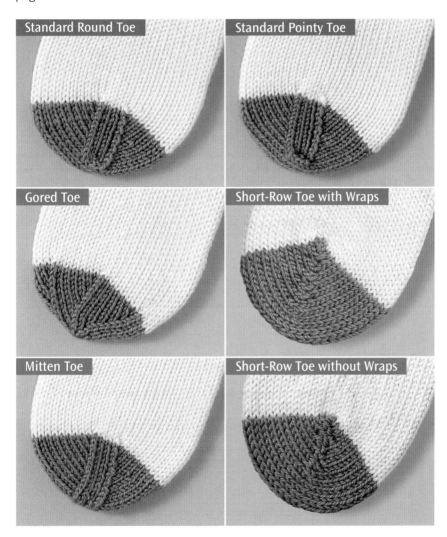

## TOE-UP SOCKS

We include three toe-up socks presenting a variety of techniques and elements. Knitting a toe-up sock involves some different techniques than the top-down approach, and yet as you can see the results are remarkably similar. We are knitting to fit a foot, after all.

Sock X begins with an easy toe (page 81). The easy toe is begun with a small rectangle of flat knitting, and then the sides are picked up to make the toe and establish the circular knitting needed for a sock. The reverse French heel (page 64) is worked in the reverse order of the top-down French heel. The gusset is worked first, and then the heel turn, followed by the heel flap. The leg and cuff are similar to working any other sock; this one is decorated with a twisted rib (page 44) and finished with the frilled bind off (page 88). In addition to being decorative, it's stretchy, enhancing the comfort of putting on and wearing the sock.

Short-row construction (page 68) is quite versatile, since you can use the same stitches for the heel or the toe. In sock Y we have used them for both. As you can see, there's no gusset. This is also an easy sock to decorate on the foot and leg, since there's no need to calculate a change in the number of stitches around the gusset. The K2, P2 rib cuff (page 43) is a good, stretchy choice for many socks, and the super-stretchy bind off (page 89) completes the sock with ease.

Judy Becker's cast on has become ubiquitous among toe-up knitters, thanks to its simplicity once learned and its durability. The standard toe is worked by increasing every other round until the desired number of stitches is reached for the foot. In sock Z, we have worked a forethought heel (page 72), which is a structure that does double duty as a standard toe (page 78). It allows you to take advantage of working the heel in the round to make bull's-eye stripes with your self-striping yarn. The cuff is worked with K1, P1 rib (page 43) and a stockinette rolled top (page 48), working just a few rounds in plain knit to produce the decorative rolled edge. The decrease bind off (versions 1 and 2 on page 88) is another variation on the standard bind offs; some knitters use it to more easily achieve a looser result.

Sock X

Sock Y

*Easy toe; reverse French heel;*
*twisted rib cuff; frilled bind off*

*Short-row toe; short-row heel;*
*K2, P2 rib cuff; super-stretchy bind off*

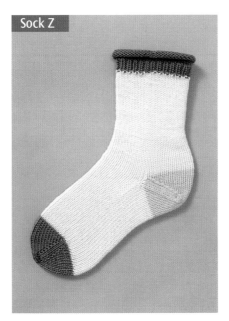

Sock Z

*Standard toe; afterthought/forethought heel;*
*ribbed cuff with stockinette rolled edge*

# Toes

One of the fundamental things to consider when choosing which toe to knit is the length of the actual toes on the foot you're knitting the sock for; another concern is the ease of working the specific toe style. As you can see from the samples below, the easy toe is the shortest toe. The short-row toe and standard toes can be lengthened or shortened by casting on fewer or more stitches. Instructions for toe-up toes begin on page 77.

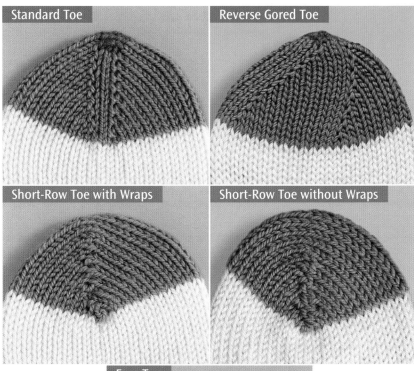

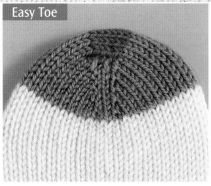

*The Sock Knitter's Handbook*

## Heels

With this group of socks, only the reverse French heel has a gusset. While simple (no stitches to pick up), there's more additional room at the ankle than with the short-row and forethought/afterthought heels. If you need to reinforce the heel area, the reverse French heel offers more possibilities than the short-row or afterthought heel. The reverse Strong heel begins with the reverse heel turn; stitches are then picked up and the heel flap and gusset areas are worked to the ankle. This is one of the simpler heel forms to work, and it offers a large area to reinforce the heel pad.

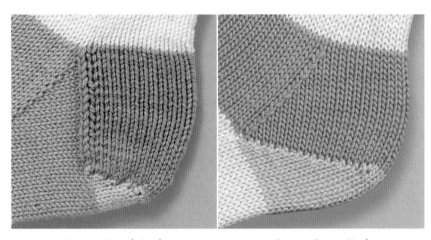

*Reverse French Heel*          *Reverse Strong Heel*

## Cuffs and Bind Offs

The cuffs are ribbed and super stretchy, but in general the issue with toe-up socks is that the bind off needs to be stretchy so you can get your heel through the cuff. See page 42 for cuff options. We have included eight bind offs for you to choose from, depending on what look you like and what type of knitting you want to do. See page 86 for bind-off options.

# 🧶 Knitting Techniques

So far we've taken a look at many options you can incorporate into your next pair of socks. In this section, we'll explain how to actually work them—from cast ons to bind offs, to knitting many types of heels and toes.

## CASTING ON FOR TOP-DOWN SOCKS

When working from the top down, you're starting with the cuff. This means the cast-on method you choose has to be flexible enough to allow your foot and heel through the opening. So, rather than a loose cast on, think "flexible."

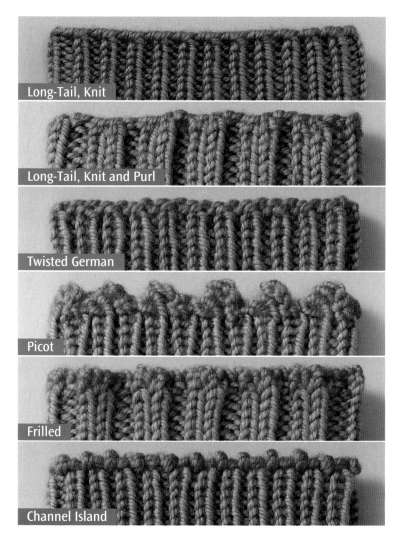

Long-Tail, Knit

Long-Tail, Knit and Purl

Twisted German

Picot

Frilled

Channel Island

Two-Color

Basic Knitted

## Long-Tail Cast On, Knit

To work, make a slipknot with a tail about four times the length of the sock circumference. Or, starting at the end of the yarn, wrap the yarn around the needle the same number of times as the stitches you're casting on; make the slipknot there. The tail is the free end, and the long end is the yarn attached to the ball. Place the slipknot on the right-hand needle. Hold both lengths of yarn in the left hand, with the tail over the thumb and the long end over the index finger. Both ends are tensioned by holding them in the palm with the other fingers (fig. 1). Insert the right-hand needle into the front of the loop on the thumb (fig. 2). Bring this yarn over the yarn on the index finger and through the loop on the thumb (fig. 3), forming a loop on the needle; tighten gently by placing the thumb under the yarn now coming from the needle and gently pulling back on it. This same motion sets up the loop on the thumb for the next stitch. Repeat this operation for the required number of stitches.

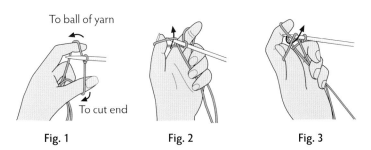

To ball of yarn

To cut end

Fig. 1              Fig. 2              Fig. 3

## Long-Tail Cast On, Knit and Purl

The typical long-tail cast on produces a knit stitch, but it's also possible to work a long-tail cast on as a purl. When you cast on in this manner for a K1, P1 rib or a K2, P2 rib, the cast-on edge becomes almost invisible, as the cast-on purled stitches recede into the purl stitches of the rib. Working the knits and purls in the cast on gives you the option to work knit and purl sequences other than K1, P1 or K2, P2, such as for a five-stitch ribbing pattern like K1, P1, K1, P2.

**To cast on in knit,** follow the directions on page 31.

**To cast on in purl,** begin as for the regular long-tail cast on, but treat the loop on the thumb like a stitch on the left-hand needle, and the yarn around the index finger like the yarn on a continental knitter's left finger when knitting. The motion of the needle and yarn is the same as making a purl stitch. Bring the needle behind the index-finger loop and through the front thumb loop (fig. 1). Then catch the index-finger yarn again and draw it through the thumb loop (fig. 2), and then under the index-finger yarn (fig. 3).

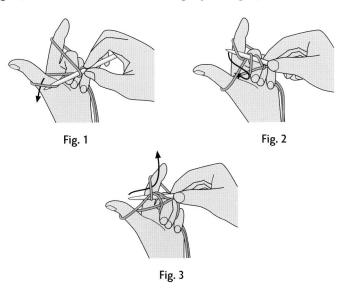

Fig. 1        Fig. 2

Fig. 3

## Twisted German Cast On (or Old Norwegian Cast On)

This method provides more elasticity than the regular long-tail cast on. Begin as long-tail cast on described previously. Put the needle under both loops of the thumb yarn (fig. 1), pointing it toward the index finger. Bring the needle back into the loop just below the thumb and up toward you (fig. 2). Twist the loop with the needle through it open so that you can scoop the index-finger yarn back through the twisted loop. The index-finger yarn is now on the needle (fig. 3). Drop the thumb loop off the thumb. Snug the yarns up against the needle. Repeat for the required number of stitches.

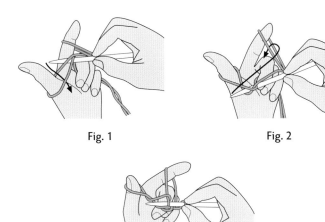

Fig. 1                    Fig. 2

Fig. 3

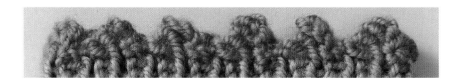

## Picot Cast On

Cast on four stitches using the basic knitted cast on (page 37) described previously, *K2, BO 1 st, K1, BO 1 st (picot made) (fig. 1), place the remaining stitch on the right-hand needle back on the left-hand needle as if to purl, cast on six stitches. Repeat from * for the desired number of stitches (fig. 2). This version gives a two-stitch picot spaced every four stitches. You can change the picot size by binding off only one stitch or as many as four stitches. The spacing is determined by the difference between the number of cast-on stitches and the number bound off.

Fig. 1                    Fig. 2

## Frilled Cast On

If you're looking for a guaranteed nonbinding top for your sock, this method is great.

Using the basic knitted cast on (page 37), cast on twice the number of stitches called for in the pattern you're working. Work two stitches together all the way around so that when you start the second round you'll have the exact number of stitches you need for your sock. For example, for K2, P2 ribbing and a 48-stitch sock, cast on 96 stitches.

**Rnd 1:** *(K2tog) twice, (P2tog) twice; rep from *.

**Rnd 2:** *K2, P2; rep from *.

Continue with your cuff.

## Channel Islands Cast On

This method is durable, and very well suited to a single rib. The double strand of yarn creates a decorative picot-like edge.

Measure a length of yarn approximately four times as long as the circumference of the sock. Fold the length of yarn in half. Make a slipknot with both strands of yarn and put it on the needle (fig. 1). Hold the tail (the doubled yarn) in your left hand, and the single yarn from the ball in your right hand. Work a yarn over with the single yarn. Wrap the tail (doubled yarn) counterclockwise around your thumb twice. Insert the right needle underneath both of the double strands of yarn that are around your thumb (fig. 2). The single strand of yarn from the previous yarn over is still held in front of the needle. Wrap the single strand of yarn around the needle as if you were knitting the stitch. Don't lose that yarn over. Pull tightly. You should have two stitches on the needle after the slipknot. The first is the yarn over, and the second is the knitted stitch you just made from the two double strands of yarn around the thumb. Repeat from * working yarn overs and knit stitches, until you have desired number of stitches (fig. 3). You'll have an odd number of stitches. It's better to have one more stitch than you need and in the first round of the cuff work the first and last stitches together.

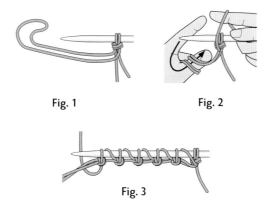

Fig. 1          Fig. 2

Fig. 3

## Two-Color Cast On

This is useful when working a corrugated rib cuff (page 45). Make a slipknot near the end of the yarn of each color and place on the needle. These two stitches do not count toward the number of stitches you need to cast on; they'll be dropped off the needle after the stitches are cast on. Holding one color on your thumb and the other color on your index finger, proceed as for long-tail cast on for the required number of stitches. The sample shown used the contrasting color on the thumb, and the main color on the index finger. You can alternate the main color on the thumb with the main color on the index finger; this gives alternating color stitches and leads directly to corrugated ribbing.

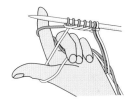

## Basic Knitted Cast On

This is a very loose and insubstantial cast on. It's best used when you're going to cast on twice the number of stitches needed and work the first row as K2tog across to yield the correct number for your sock. This is also a wonderful cast on if you're knitting a hem. The little loops of the cast on are easy to pick up and you can then knit or sew the hem in place. The hem does not bind, nor is it too tight.

To work, make a slipknot and place it on the left-hand needle. Insert the right-hand needle into the loop and knit a stitch (fig. 1); place the new stitch on the left-hand needle as if to knit (fig. 2). You now have two stitches on the left-hand needle. *Knit into the next stitch on the left-hand needle and place the stitch on the left-hand needle. Repeat from * until you have the number of stitches you need.

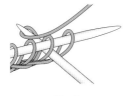

Fig. 1                    Fig. 2

## CASTING ON FOR TOE-UP SOCKS

Completely different from casting on at the cuff edge, here you need a good way to start with a few stitches that can be increased to make the toe of the sock. Following are four popular options.

## Becker Cast On

This cast on was adapted from Judy Becker's "Magic Cast On for Toe-Up Socks," which was posted on knitty.com. It can be done with double-pointed needles, but you may find it a bit easier to use one double-pointed needle and one circular needle, or two circular needles.

1.  Make a slipknot and place the loop around one of the needles; this anchor stitch will count as one stitch. Hold the needles together, with the needle that the yarn is attached to on the bottom. We'll call this needle 1 and the needle on top needle 2. For illustration purposes only, the yarn tail is light blue and the working yarn is dark blue.

2.  In your other hand, hold the yarn so that the tail goes over your index finger and the working yarn (the yarn that leads to the ball) goes over your thumb. This is the opposite of how yarn is usually held for a long-tail cast on.

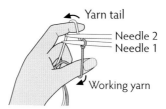

3.  Bring the tip of needle 2 (top needle) over the strand of yarn on your thumb, around and under the yarn, and back up, making a loop around needle 2; pull the loop snug, but not too tight. This is the first stitch cast on to needle 2.

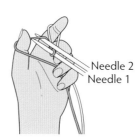

4. Bring needle 1 over the yarn tail on your index finger, around and under the yarn, and back up, making a loop around needle 1. Pull the loop snug around the needle. You've cast one stitch onto needle 1. There are now two stitches on needle 1 (the stitch you just cast on plus the slipknot).

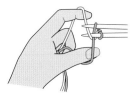

**Remember:** The top yarn (on the index finger) wraps around needle 1 (bottom needle), and the bottom yarn (the yarn around your thumb) always wraps around needle 2 (top needle).

Repeat steps 3 and 4 until you have the required number of stitches indicated in the pattern.

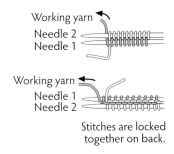

Working yarn
Needle 2
Needle 1

Working yarn
Needle 1
Needle 2

Stitches are locked together on back.

Continue as directed in the pattern, working stitches from needle 1 first and then needle 2. Work stitches on needle 2 through the back loop.

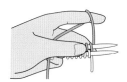

## Provisional Cast On

This technique is used in the picot-hemmed cuff (page 50), the garter-stitch sideways cuff (page 47), the lace-edge cuff (page 49), and in socks when planning for a forethought heel. It's also used when you need to pick up stitches from the cast on so that you can knit in the opposite direction. This cast on provides very little bulk, so after you pick up and knit in the opposite direction, the join is undetectable. The waste yarn is easiest to take out after the stitches have been picked up.

Work with waste yarn and a double-pointed needle in your left hand, and a crochet hook with a slipknot in your right hand. Place the double-pointed needle over the long strand held in your left hand. With the hook, draw a loop over the needle (fig. 1) and through the slipknot. Place the yarn under the needle again, *with the hook, draw a loop over the needle and through the stitch on the hook; rep from * until you have one stitch less than the number required (fig. 2). Transfer the last loop from the crochet hook to the needle after you've moved the yarn to the back of the needle. Cut the waste yarn and begin knitting with sock yarn.

Fig. 1                    Fig. 2

To remove the chain, unravel the crochet chain, placing each stitch on the needle.

## Loop-de-Loop Cast On

This cast on is easy and works beautifully when working a toe-up sock with a reverse gored toe (page 78).

1. Make a ring of yarn, and pull the tail through the ring, back to front and left to right.

2. Put the needle under the working yarn and pull a loop; first stitch cast on.

3. With the working yarn behind the ring, put the point of the needle through the ring from front to back).

4. Put the needle over the working yarn and pull a loop through the ring; second stitch cast on.

Repeat steps 2–4 until you have the desired number of stitches, always ending with step 4. After knitting the first row, pull the tail to tighten the stitches.

Without turning the needle, push the stitches to the right-hand point. Pull the working yarn from left to right and knit the stitches through the back of the loop.

## Turkish Cast On

This technique is easiest to work on two circular needles. Working from left to right, snugly wrap the working yarn counterclockwise around two needles until you have the desired number of stitches (fig. 1). Pull the bottom needle to the right so the loops are on the cable, and with the opposite end of the top needle, knit across the stitches on the top needle (fig. 2). Rotate the work and slide the stitches from the bottom needle sitting on the cable to the point of that needle. Pull the needle out of the just-worked stitches so new stitches are on now on the cable. With the opposite end of the needle, knit across the stitches on the other needle (fig. 3). Continue working on two circular needles or switch to five double-pointed needles.

Fig. 1

Fig. 2

Fig. 3

## CUFFS

The cuff is the short, usually ribbed, portion of the sock that is above the patterned leg section. Ribbing is flexible and helps the sock stay up as you wear it, but not all socks include ribbing. Shown here are several good options for working the cuff. Note that many of these cuffs can be used on both top-down and toe-up socks. It's more straightforward to use the garter-stitch sideways cuff and the lace-edge cuff for top-down socks.

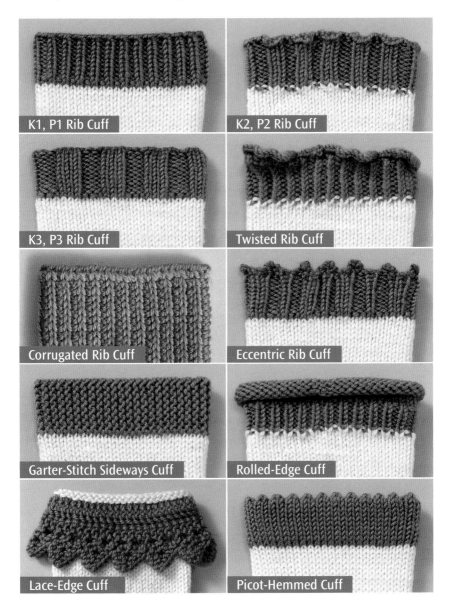

K1, P1 Rib Cuff

K2, P2 Rib Cuff

K3, P3 Rib Cuff

Twisted Rib Cuff

Corrugated Rib Cuff

Eccentric Rib Cuff

Garter-Stitch Sideways Cuff

Rolled-Edge Cuff

Lace-Edge Cuff

Picot-Hemmed Cuff

*The Sock Knitter's Handbook*

## K1, P1 Rib Cuff

The least elastic of the ribbed cuffs, the K1, P1 ribbed cuff requires an even number of stitches.

**Every rnd:** *K1, P1; rep from * around.

## K2, P2 Rib Cuff

K2, P2 ribbing is a bit more elastic than K1, P1 ribbing. This cuff requires a multiple of four stitches in the sock.

**Every rnd:** *K2, P2; rep from * around.

## K3, P3 Rib Cuff

This cuff is the most elastic of the ribbed cuffs. It requires a multiple of six stitches in the sock.

**Every rnd:** *K3, P3; rep from * around.

## Twisted Rib Cuff

The twist in the knit stitch, created by knitting through the back loop, makes this rib less elastic than a plain K1, P1. As with K1, P1, it requires an even number of stitches.

**Every rnd:** *K1tbl, P1; rep from * around.

You can make this a K2, P2 twisted rib by working *K1tbl, K1tbl, P2; rep from * around.

## Corrugated Rib Cuff

This is a decorative rib worked in two colors, starting with the two-color cast on (page 36). The knit stitches are knit with one and the purl with the other. Since there are floats that are not elastic, we recommend that you work a K1, P1 corrugated rib instead of a wider rib. When using two colors, it may be easier for you to hold the yarn for the purl in the hand that you usually use for holding the yarn when knitting with a single yarn. You need an even number of stitches for this rib, and you'll alternate the main color (MC) yarn and the contrasting color (CC) yarn. If you work the first round all in knit, there will not be the two-color purl bump from the cast-on edge.

**Rnd 1:** *K1 with MC, K1 with CC; rep from * around.

**Rnd 2:** *K1 with MC, P1 with CC; rep from * around.

Rep rnd 2 to desired length.

You can also work the corrugated rib in K2, P2 in alternating MC and CC.

## Eccentric Rib Cuff

When working a stitch pattern with a large repeat, an odd number of stitches, or an asymmetrical or irregular distribution of knits and purls, you may need to work an irregular or eccentric rib pattern to make an attractive transition from the ribbed portion of the cuff to the leg pattern. Choose the leg pattern first in order to derive the eccentric ribbing from it. Analyze the stitches in the leg pattern for its knit and purl stitches and any yarn overs, which are opportunities to do either. A ribbing results that is not regular (K3, P3) but irregular or eccentric (e.g., K2, P1, K1, P2).

In the examples below, note that the number of knit stitches is the same as the number of purl stitches, but the placement is not even. Sometimes the number of knit and purl stitches cannot be the same, but the closer they are, the more elastic the ribbing will be. For the following 16-stitch leg pattern, we created an eccentric ribbing pattern that will result in a smooth transition from the ribbing to the leg.

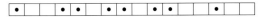

Example of uneven distribution of knits and purls

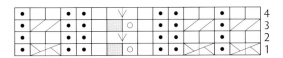

Example of eccentric rib pattern
to go with above leg pattern

| | K on RS, P on WS |
| • | P on RS, K on WS |
| ○ | YO |
| | No st |
| V | Purl into front of st and keep on needle, knit into back of st, sl both sts off needle |

| ⟋⟋ | Knit into back of second st on needle and leave st on needle, knit first st and sl both sts off needle |
| ⟍⟋ | K2tog and leave st on needle, knit first st and sl both sts off needle |

## Garter-Stitch Sideways Cuff

This cuff is knit side to side, starting with a provisional cast on (page 40). It does have some give, but is not as stretchy as others. This cuff is a good one to use when you don't know how many stitches to cast on with a new yarn. Just knit the cuff and when you're done, pick up along the edge and you'll know how many stitches you need for your sock. Or, if you do know how many stitches to cast on, work twice the number of rows, or number of garter ridges that you'll need for your sock; i.e., if you want to knit a 64-stitch sock, work 132 rows or 64 garter ridges.

Work in garter stitch with a German chain selvage as follows: Knit each stitch to the last one on the needle, and slip the last stitch as if to purl with the yarn in front. When the garter-stitch piece is long enough to fit around the calf of the wearer, graft (using garter Kitchener on page 83) the live stitches on the needle with the provisional stitches to complete the cuff.

Attach sock yarn at the seam and pick up one stitch for each chain in the selvage (pick up and knit each stitch by placing the needle under both sides of the chain, pick up the working yarn, and draw through).

After you've picked up the required number of stitches, mark beg of round and start the sock.

## Rolled-Edge Cuff

A rolled edge is added to the cuff and is an addition between cast on and cuff or between cuff and bind off for toe-up socks.

For top-down socks, use basic knitted cast on (page 37) and needles that are one or two sizes larger. Cast on the number of stitches you need for your sock. Knit around until you've knit about 1½". Change your needles to the size needed for the sock and begin the ribbed cuff you've chosen for your sock.

For a toe-up sock, after you have knit your ribbed cuff, change to needles that are one or two sizes larger than the ones you used for the cuff. Knit around for about 1½". Bind off loosely, choosing any one of the flexible bind offs on page 86.

## Lace-Edge Cuff

The lace-edge cuff is worked side to side until the length of the edging will fit around the top of the leg. Be sure to work complete eight-row repeats of the lace pattern. Start the lace edge with a provisional cast on (page 40) and join the ends with Kitchener stitch.

Provisionally CO 8 sts.

**Row 1:** Sl 1, K2, YO, ssk, K1, YO, YO, K2.

**Row 2:** Sl 1, K1, P1, K4, YO, ssk, K1.

**Row 3:** Sl 1, K2, YO, ssk, K5.

**Row 4:** Sl 1, K6, YO, ssk, K1.

**Row 5:** Sl 1, K2, YO, ssk, K1, YO, YO, ssk, YO, YO, K2.

**Row 6:** Sl 1, K1, (P1, K3) twice, YO, ssk, K1.

**Row 7:** Sl 1, K2, YO, ssk, K8.

**Row 8:** Sl 1, BO 5 sts, K4, YO, ssk, K1.

Rep rows 1–8 for patt.

For the leg, PU sts in the chain selvage. If you need to adjust the number of sts for your patt, do it in the first rnd after picking up sts.

| | K on RS, P on WS | | Sl 1 st wyib |
|---|---|---|---|
| • | P on WS, K on RS | ⊠ | BO |
| ○ | YO | | No st |
| ＼ | Ssk | | |

## Picot-Hemmed Cuff

The hemmed cuff is a doubled layer of knitting with a picot edge at the top edge. It's a firm cuff without a lot of elasticity. The tunnel created when the knitting is folded over can be threaded with elastic if needed.

Using the basic knitted cast on (page 37), cast on the total number of stitches you need for the sock. Join, being careful not to twist stitches. Work about ¾" of stockinette stitch. (Make note of how many rounds you worked.) Work one round of picot pattern as follows: *YO, K2tog; repeat from * to end. Work the same number of rounds as worked for the first ¾". Join hem as follows: With an extra double-pointed needle, pick up one stitch along the cast-on edge for every stitch cast on; knit each stitch with its corresponding live stitch. It may be easier for you to pick up one stitch at a time, depending on the weight of the yarn.

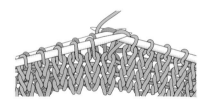

# HEELS FOR TOP-DOWN SOCKS

In most patterns, heels are worked on half of the sock's stitches. You should be able to substitute a heel if it fits you better or if you like it for the design possibilities.

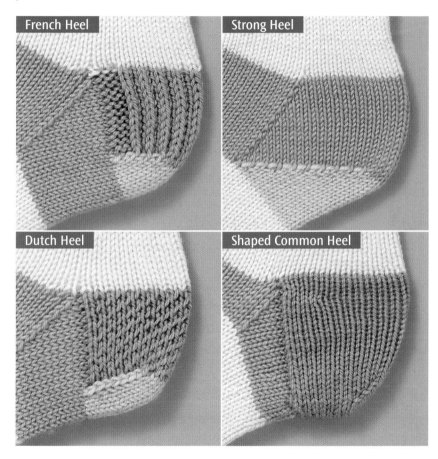

What goes into selecting a heel? One consideration is whether you'll need to pick up stitches at some point, which is a common area of difficulty. Another potential issue is fit through a high instep. As you look at the socks, notice the gussets in pink. These are an indication of how much extra space is in the sock for the instep. You can see that there's a range from the French heel to the smaller gusset.

**Heel flaps.** The flap for the French heel and Dutch heel are the same length. It's easy to lengthen a heel flap in a sock with a French heel to make the instep higher, resulting in a longer gusset, or you can extend the gusset decrease length by working more plain rounds between decreases.

In our samples on pages 18 and 19, sock A is worked in heel stitch, and sock C is worked in eye of partridge (a heel-stitch variation, described on page 56). This slipped-stitch pattern is worked to add extra durability in the heel area. The shaped common heel in sock D is longer and curves under the instep more because fewer stitches are picked up and the gusset is shorter.

**Heel turns.** Four of our five top-down socks use the heel turn—a series of short rows (rows worked back and forth on part of the active stitches, not worked to the end of the row). We'll take a closer look at those heels, viewing them from the bottom. It's very interesting to see the options we have for heels as well as for reinforcing the bottom of the foot.

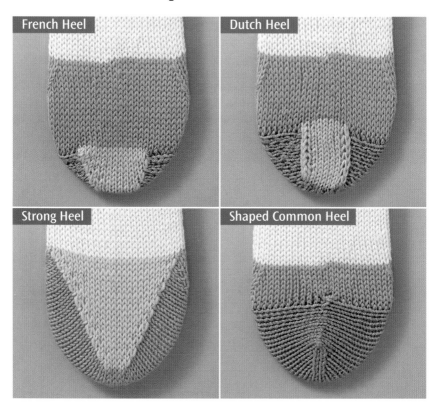

French Heel

Dutch Heel

Strong Heel

Shaped Common Heel

**The French heel** has a small trapezoid that is worked back and forth at the base of the heel flap. This creates the little piece and turns the knitting so that picking up the stitches on the side of the heel flap will be smooth with the rest of the sock.

**The Dutch heel** has a square heel turn. It's simpler to knit but tends to make the base of the heel narrower unless more stitches are allocated to the center of the heel.

The Dutch and French heels are the smallest of the four. Reinforcing thread can be used on the heel flap as well as the heel turn, which is useful if you have a sock-wear pattern at the base of your heel.

Of those with the yellow heel turn, the **Strong heel** has the largest heel turn, and instead of a heel flap, is worked with a large gusset after the leg followed by a heel turn only. There's no picking up or reverse short rows to work. This larger heel turn is good for those who need to reinforce their socks on the pad of their heels.

The **shaped common heel** does not have a heel turn. Instead, the turn is achieved by grafting the bottom of the longer heel flap and picking up stitches all around the heel. You can add reinforcing thread to the whole heel flap, which will cover more of the heel than with the French or Dutch heel.

# French Heel

Perhaps the most popular or often-used heel type in hand-knit socks, the French heel consists of a heel flap, a trapezoid worked with short rows to create the turn of the tube of fabric that will become the sock along with the gusset.

Instructions are for socks with 32 (36, 40, 44, 48, 52, 56, 60, 64, 68, 72, 76, 80, 84, 88, 92, 96) sts. The heel is worked on half the sts of the sock: 16 (18, 20, 22, 24, 26, 28, 30, 32, 34, 36, 38, 40, 42, 44, 46, 48) sts.

Start working heel flap with WS facing you. Work heel flap back and forth for 16 (18, 20, 22, 24, 26, 28, 30, 32, 34, 36, 38, 40, 42, 44, 46, 48) rows, working the pattern of your choice—see "Heel-Flap Options," opposite, for some alternatives.

**Heel Turn**
**Row 1:** Sl 1, P8 (9, 10, 11, 12, 13, 14, 15, 16, 17, 18, 19, 20, 21, 22, 23, 24), P2tog, P1. Turn.
**Row 2:** Sl 1, K3, ssk, K1. Turn.

Note that there will be a small gap between working sts that form the heel turn and unworked heel sts.

**Row 3:** Sl 1, purl to within 1 st of gap, P2tog, P1. Turn.

**Row 4:** Sl 1, knit to within 1 st of gap, K2tog, K1. Turn.

Rep rows 3 and 4 working 1 additional knit or purl st after the sl 1 until all side sts are worked, ending with completed row 4. (For some socks the last 2 rows will end with a dec—this is fine, just turn and cont.) There should be 10 (10, 12, 12, 14, 14, 16, 16, 18, 18, 20, 20, 22, 22, 24, 24, 26) sts rem on heel flap. Note that for ease of instructions, beg of rnd is now at center of bottom of foot.

Divide heel sts evenly, 5 (5, 6, 6, 7, 7, 8, 8, 9, 9, 10, 10, 11, 11, 12, 12, 13) sts onto needles 1 and 3. Needle 2 is holding instep sts.

**Needle 1:** PU 8 (9, 10, 11, 12, 13, 14, 15, 16, 17, 18, 19, 20, 21, 22, 23, 24) sts from side of heel flap, PU 2 sts at top of gusset (see page 100).

**Needle 2:** Work across instep in patt.

**Needle 3:** PU 2 sts at top of gusset, PU 8 (9, 10, 11, 12, 13, 14, 15, 16, 17, 18, 19, 20, 21, 22, 23, 24) sts from side of heel flap, knit half of heel sts.

**Sts per needle:** (15, 16, 15), (16, 18, 16), (18, 20, 18), (19, 22, 19), (21, 24, 21), (22, 26, 22), (24, 28, 24), (25, 30, 25), (27, 32, 27), (28, 34, 28), (30, 36, 30), (31, 38, 31), (33, 40, 33), (34, 42, 34), (36, 44, 36), (37, 46, 37), (39, 48, 39).

### Close Gusset Top

**Needle 1:** Knit to last 2 sts, ssk.

**Needle 2:** Work in established patt.

**Needle 3:** K2tog, knit to end.

### Gusset Decrease

**Rnd 1**

> **Needle 1:** Knit to last 3 sts, K2tog, K1.
>
> **Needle 2:** Work established patt.
>
> **Needle 3:** K1, ssk, knit to end.

**Rnd 2**

> **Needle 1:** Knit.
>
> **Needle 2:** Work established patt.
>
> **Needle 3:** Knit.

Rep rnds 1 and 2 until 32 (36, 40, 44, 48, 52, 56, 60, 64, 68, 72, 76, 80, 84, 88, 92, 96) total sts rem.

# Heel-Flap Options

Heel flaps are typically worked back and forth for a number of rows equal to half the number of stitches used for the sock. One popular fabric for the heel flap is the heel stitch. It's a slipped-stitch pattern, creating a dense, durable fabric for an area of the sock that may wear out faster than others. There are also several other choices for heel fabric: the eye of partridge stitch is also a slipped-stitch fabric that more resembles stockinette stitch, or you can use stockinette fabric as short-row heels are constructed. If you have a pattern on the leg of the sock that you really like and are going to wear the socks with clogs or sandals, why not continue the pattern down the heel?

On pages 56 and 57, you'll find instructions for heel flaps with garter edges as well as German chain selvage, given for an even number of heel stitches and an odd number of heel stitches. You may substitute these heel instructions in the pattern you're working and get back to the instructions when it comes time to turn the heel. If you've used the German chain selvage, be sure to purl the first stitch of the first row of the heel turn.

One way to work a garter-edged fabric is to knit the first three and last three stitches of every row. However, some knitters tend to go on autopilot when knitting simple stitches and they forget to knit the last three stitches.

Of the two socks with French heels shown inside out below, The one on the left is worked with three garter stitches (page 57) at the side of the heel stitch, while the one on the right is worked with a chain selvage (below). Functionally, they're the same in the number of stitches, number of stitches to pick up, and length of gusset. It's easier to pick up the stitches from the garter edge than the chain selvage. There's also less bulk on the inside of the garter-edged heel flap, which is beneficial if the wearer has tender feet.

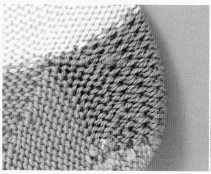 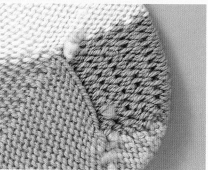

*Left, garter-edged heel flap; right, chain selvage. Notice how much less fabric is on the inside of the garter-edged heel flap. You have to really study the image to see the stitches. The sock on the right, in contrast, has a nice little line of chains, yielding more fabric than the garter alternative without being bulky.*

### Heel Stitch with German Chain Selvage

*Even number of sts in heel flap*

**Row 1 (WS):** K1, purl to last st, sl as if to purl wyif.

**Row 2:** K1, *sl 1, K1; rep from * to last st, sl 1 wyif.

*Odd number of stitches in heel flap*

**Row 1 (WS):** K1, purl to last st, sl as if to purl wyif.

**Row 2:** K1, *K1, sl 1; rep from * to last 2 sts, K1, sl 1 wyif.

### Eye of Partridge with German Chain Selvage

*Even number of sts in heel flap*

**Rows 1 and 3 (WS):** K1, purl to last st, sl as if to purl wyif.

**Row 2:** K1, *sl 1, K1; rep from * to last st, sl 1 wyif.

**Row 4:** K1, *K1, sl 1; rep from * to last 3 sts, K1, sl 1 wyib, sl 1 wyif.

*Odd number of sts in heel flap*

**Rows 1 and 3 (WS):** K1, purl to last st, sl as if to purl wyif).

**Row 2:** K1, *K1, sl 1; rep from * to last 2 sts, K1, sl 1 wyif.

**Row 4:** K1, *sl 1, K1; rep from * to last 2 sts, sl 1 wyib, sl 1 wyif.

## Heel Stitch with Garter Edge

*(Note that there's no slipped st at beg or end of any heel-flap row.)*

*Even number of sts in heel flap*

**Row 1 (WS):** K3, purl to end.

**Row 2:** P3, *sl 1, K1; rep from * to last 3 sts, K3.

*Odd number of sts in heel flap*

**Row 1:** (WS) K3, purl to end.

**Row 2:** P3, *K1, sl 1; rep from * to last 4 sts, K4.

## Eye of Partridge with Garter Edge

*Even number of sts in heel flap*

**Rows 1 and 3 (WS):** K3, purl to end.

**Row 2:** P3, *sl 1, K1; rep from * to last 3 sts, K3.

**Row 4:** P3, *K1, sl 1; rep from * to last 3 sts, K3.

*Odd number of sts in heel flap*

**Rows 1 and 3 (WS):** K3, purl to end.

**Row 2:** P3, *K1, sl 1; rep from * to last 4 sts, K4.

**Row 4:** P3, *sl 1, K1; rep from * to last 4 sts, sl 1, K3.

## Two-Color Eye of Partridge or Heel Stitch

Work two colors on the wrong side as purl one light, purl one dark. On the right side, knit the dark stitches and slip the light stitches, weaving in the light yarn so that it's on the proper side for the next wrong side row.

## Picking Up into a Chain Selvage

You have the choice of picking up both loops of the chain or just the outside loop of the chain. The fabric of the heel flap wants to curl under, so you need to unroll it to make sure you can see the whole selvage edge when you're working.

**Picking up both loops of chain.** Slip the needle under both loops of the chain and pick up a new stitch. This produces a neat edge and leaves the chain on the inside of the sock.

**Picking up outside loop of chain.** This creates a twisted, more decorative stitch, and leaves the inside of the sock the smoothest. Use a spare needle to pick up the outside loop and knit it through the back of the loop.

**Picking up into a garter selvage.** This is perhaps the easiest way to work a heel flap and gusset. Pick up the thread between the garter bumps. You'll be starting at a garter bump at the heel and begin with the thread above the bump.

## Strong Heel

The Strong heel, first published by Gerdine Crawford-Strong in the Fall 2003 issue of *Knitter's Magazine*, is a very easy and lovely heel form. The heel is worked in the round, increasing two stitches on each side until you've reached the length of the heel and a specific number of stitches. The brilliance of this heel is that you work a heel turn (like in a French heel), and when finished with the heel turn you've resumed the correct number of stitches for the sole (without picking up any stitches).

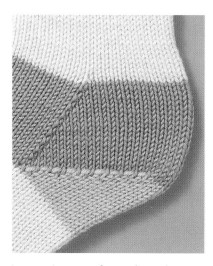

Instructions are for socks with 32 (36, 40, 44, 48, 52, 56, 60, 64, 68, 72, 76, 80, 84, 88, 92, 96) sts. Heel and gusset are worked on half the sts of the sock: 16 (18, 20, 22, 24, 26, 28, 30, 32, 34, 36, 38, 40, 42, 44, 46, 48) sts.

**Needles 1 and 2:** Instep sts.

**Needles 3 and 4:** Heel and gusset are worked on these sts.

**Rnd 1**

**Needles 1 and 2:** Work instep sts in established patt.

**Needle 3:** K1, M1, knit to end of needle.

**Needle 4:** Knit to last st, M1.

**Rnd 2**

**Needles 1 and 2:** Work in established patt.

**Needles 3 and 4:** Knit.

Rep rnds 1 and 2 for a total of 12 (14, 16, 18, 20, 22, 24, 26, 28, 30, 32, 34, 36, 38, 40, 42, 44) rnds, and needles 3 and 4 contain 28 (32, 36, 40, 44, 48, 52, 56, 60, 64, 68, 72, 76, 80, 84, 88, 92) sts each. Needles 1 and 2 contain 16 (18, 20, 22, 24, 26, 28, 30, 32, 34, 36, 38, 40, 42, 44, 46, 48) sts total.

Work heel turn as follows:
Turn the work to beg heel turn on WS row.

**Row 1 (WS):** Sl 1, P14 (16, 18, 20, 22, 24, 26, 28, 30, 32, 34, 36, 38, 40, 42, 44, 46), P2tog, P1. Turn.

**Row 2:** Sl 1, K3, ssk, K1. Turn.

**Row 3:** Sl 1, P4, P2tog, P1. Turn.

**Row 4:** Sl 1, K5, ssk, K1. Turn.

Note that there will be a small gap between working sts that form heel turn and unworked heel sts.

**Row 5:** Sl 1, purl to within 1 st of gap, P2tog, P1. Turn.

**Row 6:** Sl 1, knit to within 1 st of gap, ssk, K1. Turn.

Rep rows 5 and 6, working 1 additional knit or purl st after the sl 1 until all side sts are worked, ending with completed row 6. There should be a total of 16 (18, 20, 22, 24, 26, 28, 30, 32, 34, 36, 38, 40, 42, 44, 46, 48) sts left on heel flap, with 8 (9, 10, 11, 12, 13, 14, 15, 16, 17, 18, 19, 20, 21, 22, 23, 24) sts on each needle.

## Altering the Pattern in Strong Heel

The preceding instructions are for the basic variety of Strong heel. The original instructions call for a stockinette heel with the increases occurring at the "seam line" between sole and instep.

The chart below shows just the heel portion of the sock. This blank canvas offers opportunity to design a sock. For example, you could continue the leg pattern down to the bottom of the hee, working the pattern straight down, leaving two triangles of stockinette on the side. Or you can work a heel stitch straight down to provide some added durability if you need it.

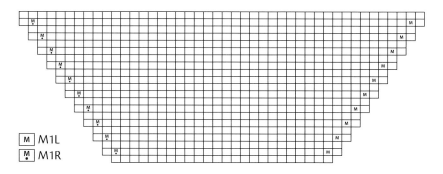

M  M1L
M  M1R

As another option for a decorative heel, you can move the position where you work the increases starting at the center back and have the increased stitches form the triangle at the heel. This allows you to continue the leg pattern down both sides of the sock—creating a nice look for those who wear socks with sandals.

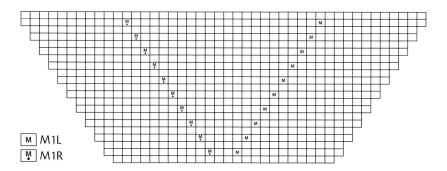

M  M1L
M  M1R

You have many options at your disposal for playing with both durability and design, simply by altering where you place the increases, which pattern stitches you work, and where you place them.

# Dutch Heel

Also known as a square heel, in this method a heel flap is worked on half the sock stitches. A straight band runs under the heel knitted on approximately one-third of the heel stitches; the width of this band can be adjusted for better fit and can be reinforced, by continuing the heel stitch or adding reinforcing thread from the heel flap. In the last (wrong side) heel-flap row, place a marker at the center of the heel flap. (For an even number of stitches, this marker will be between stitches; if odd, the marker will be the center stitch.)

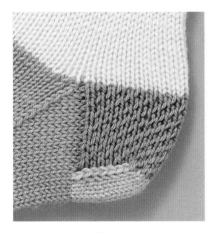

Instructions are for socks with 32 (36, 40, 44, 48, 52, 56, 60, 64, 68, 72, 76, 80, 84, 88, 92, 96) CO sts. Work heel flap on 16 (18, 20, 22, 24, 26, 28, 30, 32, 34, 36, 38, 40, 42, 44, 46, 48) sts. Work heel flap for 16 (18, 20, 22, 24, 26, 28, 30, 32, 34, 36, 38, 40, 42, 44, 46, 48) rows.

**Heel Turn**

Heel band will be 6 (6, 8, 8, 8, 10, 10, 10, 12, 12, 12, 14, 14, 14, 16, 16, 16) sts. With RS facing you,

**Row 1:** K10 (11, 13, 14, 15, 17, 18, 19, 21, 22, 23, 25, 26, 27, 29, 30, 31), K2tog, K4 (5, 5, 6, 7, 7, 8, 9, 9, 10, 11, 11, 12, 13, 13, 14, 15) sts. Turn.

**Row 2:** Sl 1, P4 (4, 6, 6, 6, 8, 8, 8, 10, 10, 10, 12, 12, 12, 14, 14, 14), P2tog. Turn.

**Row 3:** Sl 1, K4 (4, 6, 6, 6, 8, 8, 8, 10, 10, 10, 12, 12, 12, 14, 14), K2tog. Turn.

Rep rows 2 and 3 until all sts have been worked.

**Sts rem at end of heel turn:** 6 (6, 8, 8, 8, 10, 10, 10, 12, 12, 12, 14, 14, 14, 16, 16, 16).

**Gusset**

With heel needle, now needle 1, PU 8 (9, 10, 11, 12, 13, 14, 15, 16, 17, 18, 19, 20, 21, 22, 23, 24) sts along left side of heel flap. With needle 2, work across instep sts. With needle 3, PU 8 (9, 10, 11, 12, 13, 14, 15, 16, 17, 18, 19, 20, 21, 22, 23, 24) sts along right side of heel flap and work half the heel sts. **Heel sts:** 22 (24, 28, 30, 32, 36, 38, 40, 44, 46, 48, 52, 54, 56, 60, 62, 64). **Total sts in sock:** 38 (42, 48, 52, 56, 62, 66, 70, 76, 80, 84, 90, 94, 98, 104, 108, 112).

**Gusset Decrease**

**Rnd 1:** Work to last 3 sts of needle 1, K2tog, K1. With needle 2, work across instep. With needle 3, K1, ssk, knit to end.

**Rnd 2:** Work plain—knit on sole of foot and cont in patt on instep. Rep rows 1 and 2 until you have original number of sts.

# Shaped Common Heel

This heel is quite simple but requires a willingness and ability to use the Kitchener stitch. The heel flap is knit on an even number of stitches and is shaped at the back before the stitches are grafted at the bottom of the heel cup. No stitches remain from the heel. Stitches are picked up along the sides of the heel cup and only a short gusset is required to shape the transition from heel to foot.

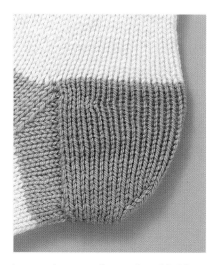

Instructions are for socks with 32 (36, 40, 44, 48, 52, 56, 60, 64, 68, 72, 76, 80, 84, 88, 92, 96) CO sts. Heel flap is worked on 16 (18, 20, 22, 24, 26, 28, 30, 32, 34, 36, 38, 40, 42, 44, 46, 48) sts and knit for 16 (18, 20, 22, 24, 26, 28, 30, 32, 34, 36, 38, 40, 42, 44, 46, 48) rows with a sl-st edge (sl last st of every row). Place a marker in the center of the sts on the last WS row.

**Row 1:** Knit to 2 sts before marker, K2tog, sl marker, ssk, knit to last st, sl 1. Turn.

**Row 2:** Purl to last st, sl 1. Turn.

Rep rows 1 and 2 for a total of 4 (6, 6, 6, 6, 8, 8, 8, 8, 10, 10, 10, 10, 12, 12, 12, 12) rows—12 (12, 14, 16, 18, 18, 20, 22, 24, 24, 26, 28, 30, 30, 32, 34, 36) sts. With RS facing you, knit to marker, half the sts rem on the other needle.

Cut yarn leaving a 20" tail and graft the sts from one needle to the sts on the other needle—6 (6, 7, 8, 9, 9, 10, 11, 12, 12, 13, 14, 15, 15, 16, 17, 18) sts to graft.

## Gusset

Beg where grafting ends at bottom of heel, with needle 1, PU 1 st to the left of the join of the graft plus 1 st in each chain at the heel-flap edge. With needle 2, work across instep. With needle 3, PU 1 st in each chain at rem heel-flap edge, ending with 1 st at right of the join of the graft. **Total sts in sock:** 38 (44, 48, 52, 56, 62, 66, 70, 74, 80, 84, 88, 92, 98, 102, 106, 110).

Resume working in the rnd.

**Rnd 1:** Work to last 3 sts of needle 1, K2tog, K1. Work across instep. With needle 3, K1, ssk, knit to end.

**Rnd 2:** Knit 1 rnd even.

Rep rnds 1 and 2 until you have original number of sts.

## HEELS FOR TOE-UP SOCKS

The function of a heel is to make the 90° turn in the tube of knitting to accommodate the wearer's heel. The instructions for the following heels will give you a sock that looks like it was knit top down. You of course have the option of knitting a top-down heel on a toe-up sock (the 90° turn is still made, the parts are just reversed).

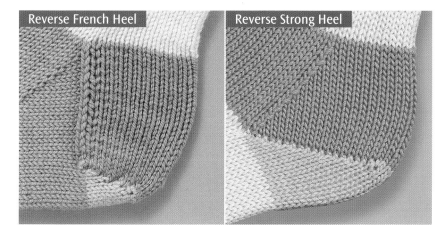

Reverse French Heel

Reverse Strong Heel

## Reverse French Heel

When finished, this heel will look like its top-down counterpart. When working, we reverse the order of parts, starting with the gusset, heel turn, and finally the heel flap.

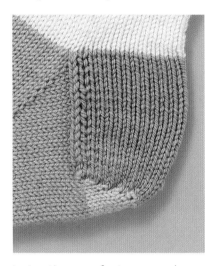

Instructions are for toe-up socks with 32 (36, 40, 44, 48, 52, 56, 60, 64, 68, 72, 76, 80, 84, 88, 92, 96) CO sts around the foot. Establish bottom of foot and top of foot. Beg of rnd is bottom of foot. Start working patt for instep on top of foot and plain stockinette on bottom of foot. Length of foot includes toe, foot, gusset, and heel turn. To calculate how long to knit the foot, measure the total length of foot and subtract the length of toe, length of gusset, and heel turn. Here is the number of rnds for the gusset and heel turn to help in your calculation: 20 (24, 24, 28, 28, 32, 32, 36, 36, 40, 40, 44, 44, 48, 48, 52, 52) rnds.

**Gusset**

**Rnd 1**

> **Needle 1:** K1, M1, knit to end.

> **Needle 2:** Knit to last st M1, K1.

> **Needle 3:** Work instep in established patt.

**Rnd 2**

> **Needles 1 and 2:** Knit.

> **Needle 3:** Work instep in established patt.

Rep rnds 1 and 2 until there are 30 (34, 36, 40, 42, 46, 48, 52, 54, 58, 60, 64, 66, 70, 72, 76, 78) sts on needles 1 and 2, and 46 (52, 56, 62, 66, 72, 76, 82, 86, 92, 96, 102, 106, 112, 116, 122, 126) sts total on all needles.

**Heel Turn**

K18 (20, 22, 24, 26, 28, 30, 32, 34, 36, 38, 40, 42, 44, 46, 48, 50), and place on holder, ssk, K8 (10, 10, 12, 12, 14, 14, 16, 16, 18, 18, 20, 20, 22, 22, 24, 24), and place next 18 (20, 22, 24, 26, 28, 30, 32, 34, 36, 38, 40, 42, 44, 46, 48, 50) sts on holder. The sole sts are in the center and on one needle. Turn.

**Row 1:** P2tog, purl across. Turn.

**Row 2:** Ssk, knit across. Turn.
Rep rows 1 and 2 until 4 sts rem, ending with WS row. You should have worked 6 (8, 8, 10, 10, 12, 12, 14, 14, 16, 16, 18, 18, 20, 20, 22, 22) rows.

## Heel Flap

Beg with a RS row, sl 1, K3, PU 6 (8, 8, 10, 10, 12, 12, 14, 14, 16, 16, 18, 18, 20, 20, 22, 22) sts along dec edge. Work across instep in established patt. PU 6 (8, 8, 10, 10, 12, 12, 14, 14, 16, 16, 18, 20, 20, 22, 22) sts along the other dec edge, knit the rest of the heel sts—16 (20, 20, 24, 24, 28, 28, 32, 32, 36, 36, 40, 40, 44, 44, 48, 48) sts on needle 1. Work across instep in established patt.

**Row 1:** Sl 1, K14 (16, 18, 20, 22, 24, 26, 28, 30, 32, 34, 36, 38, 40, 42, 44, 46), ssk last st with the first st on the holder. Turn.

**Row 2:** Sl 1, P14 (16, 18, 20, 22, 24, 26, 28, 30, 32, 34, 36, 38, 40, 42, 44, 46), purl last st tog with first st on holder. Turn.

Rep rows 1 and 2 until you have 1 st left on each holder, ending with a WS row.

## Leg

Beg with RS, sl 1, K14 (14, 18, 18, 22, 22, 26, 26, 30, 30, 34, 34, 38, 38, 42, 42, 46), knit st off holder.

This is now beg of rnd.

Work established patt on leg; work last st off holder when you come to it.

# Reverse Strong Heel

This heel starts with the heel turn in reverse and finishes off with the gusset and heel flap. You have the opportunity of using reinforcement on the heel turn. These instructions are for two circular needles. If working with double-pointed needles, place half the stitches for needle 1 on two double-pointed needles; place the stitches for needle 2 on another two double-pointed needles. When working instructions for needle 1, work needles 1 and 2. For needle 2 in the instructions, work needles 3 and 4.

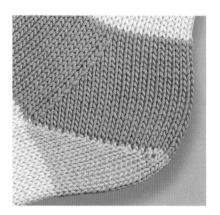

Instructions are for toe-up socks with 32 (36, 40, 44, 48, 52, 56, 60, 64, 68, 72, 76, 80, 84, 88, 92, 96) sts around the foot. Establish bottom of foot and top of foot. Beg of rnd is bottom of foot. Start working patt for instep on top of foot and plain stockinette on bottom of foot. Work to desired foot length minus length of toe and length of heel. Work heel turn on 16 (18, 20, 22, 24, 26, 28, 30, 32, 34, 36, 38, 40, 42, 44, 46, 48) sts on bottom of sock only.

**Row 1:** P2tog, purl across. Turn.

**Row 2:** Ssk, knit across. Turn.

Rep rows 1 and 2 until 4 sts rem, ending with WS row. You should have worked 12 (14, 16, 18, 20, 22, 24, 26, 28, 30, 32, 34, 36, 38, 40, 42, 44) rows.

Beg with a RS row, sl 1, K3, PU 12 (14, 16, 18, 20, 22, 24, 26, 28, 30, 32, 34, 36, 38, 40, 42, 44) sts along dec edge. Work across instep in established patt. PU 12 (14, 16, 18, 20, 22, 24, 26, 28, 30, 32, 34, 36, 38, 40, 42, 44) sts along the other dec edge, knit the rest of the heel sts—28 (32, 36, 40, 44, 48, 52, 56, 60, 64, 68, 72, 76, 80, 84, 88, 92) sts on needle 1. Work across instep in established patt.

Beg working in rnds in established patt on instep, and work gusset dec on sole and heel sts as follows.

**Rnd 1**

　**Needle 1 (heel sts):** K1, ssk, knit to last 3 sts, K2tog, K1.

　**Needle 2 (instep):** Work in established patt.

**Rnd 2**

　**Needle 1:** Knit.

　**Needle 2:** Work in established patt.

Rep rnds 1 and 2 until you have 32 (36, 40, 44, 48, 52, 56, 60, 64, 68, 72, 76, 80, 84, 88, 92, 96) sts (the original you started with). If you have a high instep, you may want to work rnd 1, rnd 2, rnd 2 to extend the length of the heel and gusset. Work leg the length you desire with cuff and BO.

# HEELS FOR TOE-UP OR TOP-DOWN SOCKS

Some types of heels can be used for either toe-up or top-down socks, such as short-row heels and the forethought and afterthought heels.

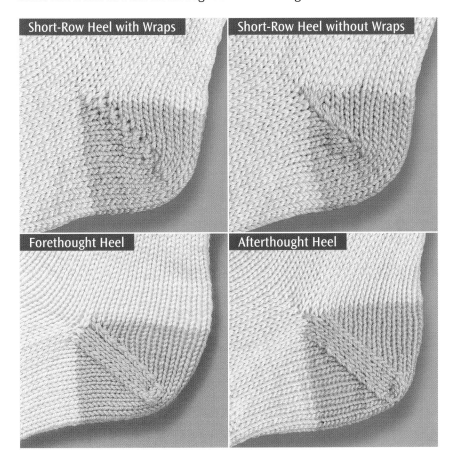

Short-Row Heel with Wraps

Short-Row Heel without Wraps

Forethought Heel

Afterthought Heel

## Short-Row Heel with Wraps

This heel is worked using half the number of stitches of the sock. The short-row sequence is worked until you have about 20% of the total stitches for the sock unwrapped. Do the calculation first. Multiply the total number needed by 0.2, and then round to the nearest even number. If you have an odd number of stitches in the heel, the number of unwrapped stitches should be odd. If the heel is worked on an even number of stitches, the number of unwrapped stitches should be even.

Instructions for socks with 32 (36, 40, 44, 48, 52, 56, 60, 64, 68, 72, 76, 80, 84, 88, 92, 96) sts around the foot. Arrange sts so that half the sts are on 1 needle, and work those sts only for the short-row heel: 16 (18, 20, 22, 24, 26, 28, 30, 32, 34, 36, 38, 40, 42, 44, 46, 48) sts.

**Row 1:** K14 (16, 18, 20, 22, 24, 26, 28, 30, 32, 34, 36, 38, 40, 42, 44, 46) sts, yf, sl next st as if to purl, yb, sl wrapped st pwise back to LH needle. Last st is unwrapped; 2nd st is wrapped on RH needle and remains unworked. Turn.

**Row 2:** P12 (14, 16, 18, 20, 22, 24, 26, 28, 30, 32, 34, 36, 38, 40, 42, 44), yb, sl next st as if to purl, yf, sl wrapped st back to LH needle. Last st is unworked and unwrapped; 2nd st is wrapped and unworked. Turn.

**Row 3:** Knit across to st before last wrapped st, yf, sl next st, yb, sl wrapped st back to LH needle, turn. Knit st tog with both wraps as follows: Sl knit st to RH needle as if to purl, PU wraps with LH needle and place on RH needle, sl all 3 back to LH needle as if to purl and K3tog, yf, sl next st as if to purl, yb, sl st back to LH needle. Turn.

**Row 4:** Purl across to st before last wrapped st, yb, sl next st, yf, return slipped st to LH needle. Turn.

Rep rows 3 and 4 until 6 (6, 8, 8, 10, 10, 10, 12, 12, 14, 14, 14, 16, 16, 18, 18, 18) sts rem unwrapped. End ready for a RS row.

 The Sock Knitter's Handbook

### Reverse Short-Row Shaping:

Your short rows will be more attractive if you sl the wrap up and over the st before knitting it together with its st.

**Row 1:** Knit across to next wrapped st. Knit st tog with wrap as follows: yf, sl next st as if to purl, yb, sl wrapped st back to LH needle. Turn. This st now has 2 wraps.

**Row 2:** Purl across to next wrapped st . Purl st tog with wrap as follows: Sl st, place wrap on RH needle, sl both to LH needle as if to purl. Purl st tog with wrap through back loop (needle entering on back of work from left to right), yb, sl next st to RH needle, yf, return st to LH needle. Turn.

**Row 3:** Knit across to next wrapped st. Knit st tog with both wraps as follows: Sl knit st to RH needle as if to purl, PU wraps with LH needle and place on RH needle, sl all 3 back to LH needle as if to purl and K3tog, yf, sl next st as if to purl, yb, sl st back to LH needle. Turn.

**Row 4:** Purl to next wrapped st. Purl st tog with wrap as follows: Sl st to RH needle, PU 2 wraps from base of st and place on RH needle over first st slipped, sl them back one at a time as if to purl to LH needle and P3tog through back loop. Wrap next st. For rest of shaping, you'll add a second wrap to each st.

Rep rows 3 and 4 until you've worked all wrapped sts. When you've worked last wrapped st on RS, wrap last st, turn and purl to last wrapped st on side. Purl wrapped st with its wraps as above, wrap last st. Turn.

The heel is now finished, and you have both end sts wrapped.

With heel-st yarn, knit across the heel, knitting wrap with last st of heel. Work across instep, when you get back to heel sts, knit first heel st with wrap.

## Short-Row Heel without Wraps

This version of unwrapped short rows is used with permission from Carol Wulster and Sock Wizard software.

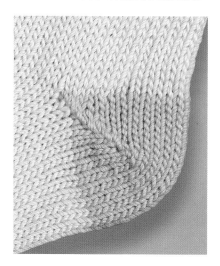

**Sl 1:** Sl 1 st pw.

**KCGS:** Sl next st kw. Insert right needle purlwise in the right leg of the st on row below slipped st on the left needle. Insert left needle in front of first two sts on right needle and K2tog. KCGS complete.

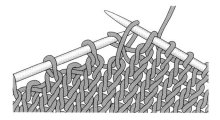

**PCGS:** Sl next st pw. Insert right needle from top to bottom in purl bump on row below the slipped st on the left needle. Insert left needle in back of first two sts on right needle and P2tog. PCGS complete.

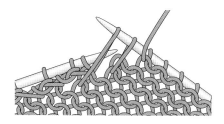

Instructions are for socks with 32 (36, 40, 44, 48, 52, 56, 60, 64, 68, 72, 76, 80, 84, 88, 92, 96) sts around foot. Arrange sts so that half of the sts are on 1 needle, and work those sts only for the short-row heel: 16 (18, 20, 22, 24, 26, 28, 30, 32, 34, 36, 38, 40, 42, 44, 46, 48) sts.

**Row 1:** K15 (17, 19, 21, 23, 25, 27, 29, 31, 33, 35, 37, 39, 41, 43, 45, 47). Turn.

**Row 2:** Sl 1, P13 (15, 17, 19, 21, 23, 25, 27, 29, 31, 33, 35, 37, 39, 41, 43, 45). Turn.

**Row 3:** Sl 1, K12 (14, 16, 18, 20, 22, 24, 26, 28, 30, 32, 34, 36, 38, 40, 42, 44). Turn.

Cont working 1 st less each row before turning until you've worked sl 1, P9 (9, 11, 11, 13, 13, 13, 15, 15, 17, 17, 19, 19, 19, 21, 21, 21). Turn.

**Reverse Short-Row Shaping**
**Row 1:** Sl 1, K7 (7, 9, 9, 11, 11, 11, 13, 13, 15, 15, 17, 17, 17, 19, 19, 19), KCGS. Turn.

**Row 2:** S1 1, P5 (5, 7, 7, 9, 9, 9, 11, 11, 13, 13, 15, 15, 15, 17, 17, 17), PCGS. Turn.

**Row 3:** Sl 1, knit 1 st more than row 2 above, KCGS. Turn.

**Row 4:** Sl 1, purl 1 st more than row 3 above, PCGS. Turn.

Cont working 1 st more on each row before KCGS or PCGS until you've worked the following: Sl 1, K12 (14, 16, 18, 20, 22, 24, 26, 28, 30, 32, 34, 36, 38, 40, 42, 44), KCGS, K1. Turn.

**Complete Heel**
**Row 1:** Sl 1, purl to end.

**Row 2:** Sl 1, knit to end.

Beg working in rnds by joining to first instep st.

## Forethought Heel

This heel is functionally the same as a peasant or afterthought heel. It gives you the option of working it as you knit the rest of the sock, rather than knitting it at the end. By using different yarn or yarn from the other end of the ball, you can knit the heel, and then resume, maintaining the patterning.

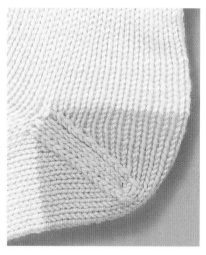

**Rnd 1:** K1, ssk, knit to last 3 sts of provisional CO, K2tog, K1. Rep on other side of heel.

**Rnd 2:** Knit around entire heel.

Rep rnds 1 and 2 until you have 20% of sts of sock.

Graft stitches together with Kitchener stitch.

Pick up stitches from instep that were placed on holder.

With scrap yarn, and a spare needle, provisionally cast on half the number of stitches of the sock or the number you want for the heel. Place spare needle so that you're ready to knit just the cast-on stitches instead of the instep. Take yarn from other side of skein. If you're using hand-painted yarn, locate the part of the painted pattern you're currently working in and start using that. The heel will cont in this pattern and form concentric circles of pattern, thus it's sometimes called a bull's-eye heel.

Knit across these stitches. Join with heel stitches and knit across heel stitches.

Unzip provisional cast on and pick up the provisionally cast-on stitches. Many times you may pick up one less st than you cast on. If that is the case, just pick up an extra stitch where it looks like you need one. Start working pattern where you left off with sock yarn on instep. Work heel and bottom of foot in stockinette stitch. When you reach side of sock, pick up two stitches in corner, such as at gusset (page 100). The extra two stitches should be on heel needle. Knit across heel. At next corner, pick up two stitches at heel to close gap. Continue working established pattern. Working across heel stitches, knit first two and last two stitches together until the original number of heel stitches remains. Continue pattern on instep and stockinette stitch on sole to desired heel-to-toe length.

# Afterthought Heel

Sometimes called a peasant heel, this looks like the forethought heel; however, you knit it after working the rest of the sock, not at the same time. This heel can be worked on any number of stitches.

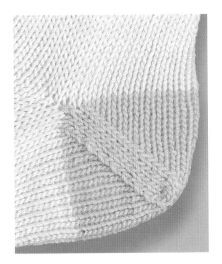

**Begin Heel Preparation**

Knit first two stitches of the round. With waste yarn, knit to within two stitches of seam line. Break off waste yarn.

Slide the stitches back to beginning of round (where the waste yarn begins—don't reknit the two seam stitches). Continue knitting in the round with the full pattern.

Work the sock to the toe and finish the toe.

**Shape the Heel**

Carefully pick up the stitches that have waste yarn holding them. You should have the same number on the leg side as the foot side. Unpick the waste yarn. Divide the stitches onto four double-pointed needles (or two circulars, or three double points with one half on one needle and a quarter on the other two). Occasionally when picking up the stitches from waste yarn you'll have one more or one fewer stitch than you need. Adjust the stitch count in the first knit round.

Knit 1 rnd.

**Rnd 1:** K1, ssk, knit to last 3 sts, K2tog, K1. Rep on other side of heel.

**Rnd 2:** Knit around entire heel.

Rep rnds 1 and 2 until you have 20% of original sock sts.

Graft sts tog with Kitchener st (page 82).

# TOES FOR TOP-DOWN SOCKS

When deciding what kind toe to knit, consider fit, technique, and design. Choose the option that makes sense for the length of the wearer's toes. Standard round and pointy toes are both relatively simple techniques, and both finish with Kitchener grafting or a three-needle bind off. You can change the length of the toe by varying the number of plain knitted rounds worked between decrease rounds. A gored toe, worked from the top down, is simple to work and finish. You run the yarn through the last stitches like you would for the top of a hat. The toe can be worked to be shorter or longer based on the number of plain knitted rounds between decrease rounds. The mitten toe has the same structure as the standard toe. Selecting which stitches to graft together provides its distinctive look. Use this toe if you like its distinct appearance.

Another alternative is to work a short-row toe to match the heel. This toe tends to be shorter than the standard toe, so it's important to make sure that the whole sock is long enough before starting the toe. For a top-down sock, short-row toes are finished with Kitchener grafting or a Greek bind off.

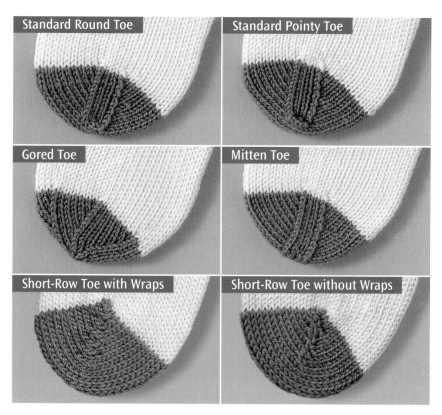

| Standard Round Toe | Standard Pointy Toe |
| Gored Toe | Mitten Toe |
| Short-Row Toe with Wraps | Short-Row Toe without Wraps |

## Standard Toe

This is one of the most commonly used toes. Instructions are written assuming you're using four double-pointed needles—needle 1 holds half the total stitches (either top or bottom) and needles 2 and 3 each hold one-quarter of the total stitches.

**Rnd 1**

**Needle 1:** K1, ssk, knit to last 3 sts, K2tog, K1.

**Needle 2:** K1, ssk, knit to end.

**Needle 3:** Knit to last 3 sts, K2tog, K1.

**Rnd 2:** Knit around.

**For standard round toe**

Rep rnds 1 and 2 until you have half of the original sts of your sock.

Rep rnd 1 only until you have one-quarter of the original sts of your sock. Graft using Kitchener st (page 82).

**For standard pointy toe**

Work rnds 1 and 2 until you have one-quarter of the sts you started with; this will give you a longer toe. Graft using Kitchener st (page 82).

## Gored Toe

This style of toe has the decreases evenly spaced around the sock.

For a four-gored or star toe, make sure that the number of stitches you have is evenly divisible by four. Knit one round, increasing or decreasing to get the proper number of stitches before working the toe. Decrease four times evenly spaced every other round until you have eight stitches left. Cut yarn, leaving a 12" tail. Thread tail onto darning needle and pull through remaining stitches firmly.

For a six-gored toe, make sure your stitch count is evenly divisible by six. Arrange stitches on double-pointed needles or place markers to make decreasing at the same place easier. Decrease six times evenly on every other round until you have six stitches left. Cut yarn, leaving a 12" tail. Thread tail onto darning needle and pull through remaining stitches firmly.

## Mitten Toe

Much of the technique for this toe is similar to the standard toe. It can be quite decorative if you're working a fancy pattern on the toe.

The decreases are worked up to the tip of the toe, allowing for decoration of the toe to the tip as well as offering a continuous band around the side of the foot for a different look.

Begin as for the standard toe, but continue decreasing until only eight stitches remain, ending at the center of the sole. Combine the next four stitches on one needle and the following four stitches on a second needle. Graft using Kitchener stitch (page 82); this graft will be perpendicular to the direction in which one usually grafts the toe.

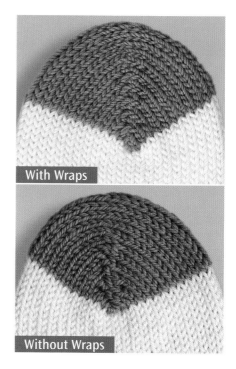

With Wraps

Without Wraps

## Short-Row Toe

The short-row toe can also be used on a top-down sock. Arrange the stitches so that all the sole stitches are on one needle, and the instep stitches are on two double-pointed needles, on a holder, or on a circular needle. Begin working short-row toe instructions (with or without wraps on pages 79 and 80) at row 1. When finished (ignore the information about picking up stitches from provisional cast on), graft the stitches from the toe to the instep using Kitchener stitch (page 82) or the zigzag bind off (page 85).

## TOES FOR TOE-UP SOCKS

As for top-down toes, consider fit, technique, and design when deciding what kind of toe to knit.

The standard toe, worked toe up, is now simpler with Judy Becker's cast on. You can change the length of the toe by varying the number of cast-on stitches. Cast on fewer stitches and you'll have a longer toe that would fit a pointy foot better, while those with shorter toes might want to cast on more stitches. This is one of the more popular toe-up toes.

The reverse gored toe uses a loop-de-loop cast on; it can be challenging to have six or eight stitches on several needles without any knitting to stabilize it. It becomes simpler once you have worked a few rounds to support the needles. A short-row toe requires a longer provisional cast on along with the short rows to work. Depending on the number of stitches you start with, the short-row toe can be lengthened or shortened. The easy toe tends to be shorter than the standard toe and about the same length as the short-row toe. It starts with a small rectangle worked back and forth; then stitches are picked up around all the sides. After that, it's simply worked like a standard toe.

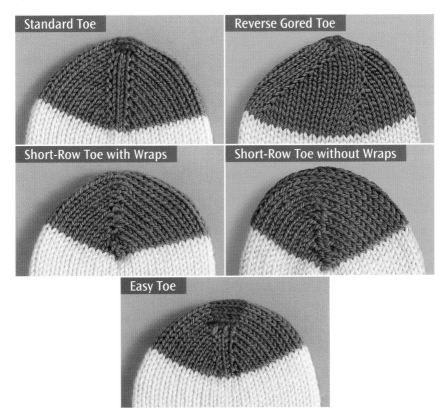

## Standard Toe

Using the Becker cast on (page 38) or the Turkish cast on (page 41), cast on 20% of the stitches needed for the sock. (Multiply the total number needed by 0.2 and then round to the nearest even number.) Knit one round. Divide stitches with markers or on multiple double-pointed needles.

**Rnd 1**

    **Needle 1:** K1, M1, knit to last st of first half, M1, K1.

    **Needle 2:** K1, M1, knit to last st of first half, M1, K1.

**Rnd 2:** Knit around.

Rep rnds 1 and 2 until you have the number of sts you need for your sock.

## Reverse Gored Toe

Using the loop-de-loop cast on (page 40), cast on six stitches for a six-gored toe or eight stitches for a four-gored toe or star toe. Arrange on two circular or double-pointed needles.

**Four-Gored Toe**

**Rnd 1:** *K2, M1; rep from * around (12 sts).

**Rnd 2 and all even rnds:** Knit.

**Rnd 3:** *K3, M1; rep from * around (16 sts)

Cont patt, working 1 more knit st before the M1 on odd-numbered rnds, until you have the desired number of sts for your sock.

**Six-Gored Toe**

**Rnd 1:** *K1, M1; rep from * around (12 sts).

**Rnd 2 and all even rnds:** Knit.

**Rnd 3:** *K2, M1; rep from * around (18 sts).

Cont patt, working 1 more knit st before the M1 on odd-numbered rnds, until you have the desired number of sts for your sock.

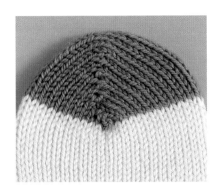

## Short-Row Toe with Wraps

This is the traditional version of a short-row toe, which most resembles the toe on a commercial sock.

Instructions are for toe-up socks with 32 (36, 40, 44, 48, 52, 56, 60, 64, 68, 72, 76, 80, 84, 88, 92, 96) sts around the foot.

Using waste yarn and provisional CO (see page 40), CO 16 (28, 20, 22, 24, 26, 28, 30, 32, 34, 36, 38, 40, 42, 44, 46, 48 sts. Change to sock yarn and purl 1 row.

**Row 1 (RS):** K15 (17, 19, 21, 23, 25, 27, 29, 31, 33, 35, 37, 39, 41, 43, 45, 47), yf, sl next st, yb, sl wrapped st back to LH needle. Turn.

**Row 2:** P14 (16, 18, 20, 22, 24, 26, 28, 30, 32, 34, 36, 38, 40, 42, 44, 46), yb, sl next st, yf, sl wrapped st back to LH needle. Turn.

Beg short-row shaping, sl all sts pw.

**Row 3:** Knit to st before last wrapped st, yf, sl next st, yb, sl wrapped st back to LH needle. Turn.

**Row 4:** Purl to st before last wrapped st yb, sl next st, yf, sl wrapped st back to LH needle. Turn.

Rep rows 3 and 4 until 6 (6, 8, 8, 10, 10, 10, 12, 12, 14, 14, 14, 16, 16, 18, 18, 18) sts remain unwrapped, end by working WS row.

**Reverse Short-Row Shaping**

Note that your short rows will be more attractive if you sl the wrap up and over the st before knitting it tog with the st.

**Row 1 (RS):** Knit to next wrapped st, knit this st tog with wrap, yf, sl next st, yb, sl wrapped st back to LH needle. Turn. This st now has 2 wraps.

**Row 2:** Purl to next wrapped st, purl this st tog with wrap, yb, sl next st to RH needle, yf, return st to LH needle. Turn.

**Row 3:** Knit to next wrapped st, sl knit st to RH needle as if to purl, PU wraps with LH needle and place on RH needle, sl all 3 sts back to LH needle as if to purl, K3tog, yf, sl next st pw, yb, sl st back to LH needle. Turn.

**Row 4:** Purl to next wrapped st, sl purl st kw, PU 2 wraps from base of st and place on RH needle over first slipped st, sl them back one at a time pw to LH needle, P3tog through the back of the loops, yb, sl next st pw, yf, sl st back to LH needle turn.

Rep rows 3 and 4 until you've worked all double-wrapped sts.

The 2 end sts have 1 wrap each. Beg knitting in rnd, with RS facing you. Knit across, knitting the end sts with their wraps. Undo the provisional CO, PU 16 (18, 20, 22, 24, 26, 28, 30, 32, 34, 36, 40, 42, 44, 46, 48) sts, and begin working in the round for the foot.

## Short-Row Toe without Wraps

This version is used with permission from Carol Wulster and Sock Wizard Software.

**Sl 1:** Sl 1 st pw.

**KCGS:** Sl next st kw. Insert right needle pw in right leg of st on row below sl st on left needle. Insert left needle in front of first 2 sts on right needle and K2tog. KCGS complete. See page 70.

**PCGS:** Sl next st pw, insert right needle from top to bottom in purl bump on row below sl st on left needle. Insert left needle in back of first 2 sts on right needle and P2tog. PCGS complete. See page 70.

Instructions are for toe-up socks with 32 (36, 40, 44, 48, 52, 56, 60, 64, 68, 72, 76, 80, 84, 88, 92, 96) sts around foot.

**Toe Cast On and Shaping**
**Needle 1:** Provisionally CO (page 40) 16 (18, 20, 22, 24, 26, 28, 30, 32, 34, 36, 38, 40, 42, 44, 46, 48) sts.

**Row 1:** P16 (18, 20, 22, 24, 26, 28, 30, 32, 34, 36, 38, 40, 42, 44, 46, 48). Turn.

**Row 2:** Sl 1, knit until last st (1 st is left on the needle). Turn.

**Row 3:** Sl 1, purl until last st (1 st is left on the needle). Turn.

**Row 4:** Sl 1, knit to last unworked st. Turn.

**Row 5:** Sl 1, purl to last unworked st. Turn.

Cont working 1 st more each row before KCGS or PCGS until you've worked the following: Sl 1, P9 (9, 11, 11, 13, 13, 13, 15, 15, 17, 17, 19, 19, 19, 21, 21, 21). Turn.

**Turn Toe**
**Row 1:** Sl 1, K7 (7, 9, 9, 11, 11, 11, 13, 13, 15, 15, 17, 17, 17, 19, 19, 19), KCGS. Turn.

**Row 2:** S1 1, P5 (5, 7, 7, 9, 9, 9, 11, 11, 13, 13, 15, 15, 15, 17, 17, 17), PCGS. Turn.

**Row 3:** Sl 1, knit 1 st more than row above, KCGS. Turn.

**Row 4:** Sl 1, purl 1 st more than row above, PCGS. Turn.

Cont working 1 st more each row before KCGS or PCGS until you've worked the following: Sl 1, K12 (14, 16, 18, 20, 22, 24, 26, 28, 30, 32, 34, 36, 38, 40, 42, 44), KCGS, K1. Turn.

**Row 1:** Sl 1, purl to end.

**Row 2:** Sl 1, knit to end.

**Foot**
With free needle, PU 16 (18, 20, 22, 24, 26, 28, 30, 32, 34, 36, 38, 40, 42, 44, 46, 48) provisional CO sts. Beg of rnd.

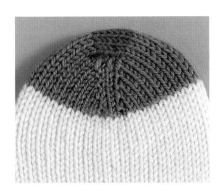

## Easy Toe

This construction consists of a small stockinette knit square; you then pick up stitches all the way around and increase to the number of stitches you need for the sock.

With waste yarn, provisionally cast on 20% of the total number of stitches you need for your sock pattern. (Multiply the total number needed by 0.2 and then round to the nearest even number.) If you want a longer toe, choose the smaller number. If you want a shorter toe, pick the larger number. Change to sock yarn and purl one row. Work back and forth in stocki-nette stitch for six rows, ending with a purl row. The needle with the stitches on it is needle 1.

Unzip provisional cast-on stitches and place stitches on a spare needle. Begin knitting in the round. With right side facing, knit the stitches on needle 1 (seventh row from above). With same needle pick up and knit two stitches from side of rectangle.

With needle 2, pick up and knit two stitches from side of rectangle and knit half the stitches on the next long side of the rectangle. With needle 3, knit the second half of the sts.

On the long side, pick up and knit two stitches from the last short side of rectangle. With needle 4, pick up and knit two stitches from short side, and then start knitting on the long side.

Look at the stitches on the needles. There will be four increases worked every other round. The increase takes place between the end two stitches on the short side of the rectangle, and you increase until you have the proper number of stitches for your sock.

# BIND OFFS FOR TOP-DOWN SOCKS

When working a sock from the top down, there are several bind-off techniques for closing the toe, depending on the style of toe worked.

## Kitchener Stitch for Stockinette Stitch

Use this technique to sew the ends of a stockinette-stitch toe together. Work with the two pieces on the needles with wrong sides together, one needle behind the other. Thread a yarn needle with the yarn attached to the back knitting needle and work as follows.

Insert the yarn needle into the first stitch of the front needle as if to purl, pull the yarn through but leave the stitch on the knitting needle. Being careful to take the yarn under the knitting needle each time, insert the yarn needle into the first stitch on the back needle as if to knit, pull the yarn through but leave the stitch on the knitting needle.

*Insert the yarn needle into the first stitch of the front needle as if to knit, then slip this stitch off the knitting needle. Insert the yarn needle into the next stitch of the front needle as if to purl, pull the yarn through but leave the stitch on the knitting needle.

Insert the yarn needle into the first stitch of the back needle as if to purl, then slip this stitch off the knitting needle. Insert the yarn needle through the next stitch of the back needle as if to knit, pull the yarn through but leave this stitch on the knitting needle.*

Repeat from * to * until all stitches are joined. Do not draw the yarn too tightly. The stitches should have the same tension as the knitted stitches. Fasten the end securely.

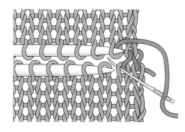

Here's a shorthand way of remembering how the grafting is done:

**Front needle:** Knit off, purl on.

**Back needle:** Purl off, knit on.

# Kitchener Stitch for Garter Stitch

Use this technique when you want to graft the toe of a garter-stitch sock. Begin with the work on the *front* needle ending with a *wrong-side row,* and the *back* needle ending with a *right-side row.* Place the two pieces on the needles with wrong sides held together, one needle behind the other. Thread a yarn needle with yarn attached to the back knitting needle and work as follows.

Insert yarn needle into the first stitch of the front needle as if to purl (fig. 1), and pull the yarn through but leave the stitch on the knitting needle. Being careful to take the yarn under the knitting needle each time, insert the yarn needle into the first stitch of the back needle as if to purl, and pull the yarn through but leave the stitch on the knitting needle.

*Insert the yarn needle into the first stitch of the front needle as if to knit (fig. 2), and then slip this stitch off the needle. Insert the yarn needle into the next stitch of the front needle as if to purl, and pull the yarn through but leave the stitch on the knitting needle.

Insert the yarn needle into the first stitch of the back needle as if to knit (fig. 3). Take this stitch off and onto the yarn needle. Put the yarn needle through the next stitch of the back needle as if to purl, and pull the yarn through, but leave this stitch on the knitting needle.*

Repeat from * to * until one stitch remains on each needle. Insert a tapestry needle into the last stitch of the front needle as if to knit and take this st off the needle. Insert the yarn needle into the first stitch of the back needle as if to knit and take this st off the needle. Don't draw the yarn too tightly. The stitches should have the same tension as the knitted stitches. Fasten end securely.

Shorthand for grafting:

**Front needle:** Knit off, purl on.

**Back needle:** Knit off, purl on.

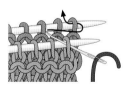

Fig. 1

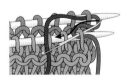

Fig. 2

Fig. 3

# Three-Needle Bind Off

When binding off the top and bottom toe stitches together, this method creates a seam between them. You have the choice of working the bind off with the chain on the outside or inside. (Working with chain on the inside will be attractive, but since it may rub on the tips of the toes, working with the chain on the outside may be more comfortable.) To avoid a puckering bound-off edge, use a larger third needle to bind off the stitches.

You can hold the stitches with right sides facing each other (you'll have to turn the sock inside out to do this), in which case the bind off will not show on the right side. Or with wrong sides facing each other, in which case the bind off will show on the right side. The first two needles are holding these stitches. With the third needle, work as follows.

*Insert knitwise into the first stitch on the front needle and at the same time knitwise into the first stitch on the back needle (fig. 1). Wrap as for a knit stitch and draw the working yarn through both stitches to make one stitch which is now on the larger, right-hand needle.*

Repeat from * to * so that there are two stitches on the right-hand needle.

**Using the tip of one of the needles in your left hand, lift the first stitch worked over the second stitch worked—just like regular binding off!**

Work one more stitch (knitting one stitch from both front and back needle), then repeat from ** to ** (fig. 2).

Fig. 1

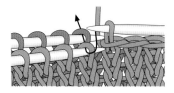

Fig. 2

## Gathered or Hat-Top Bind Off

An alternative to grafting or Kitchener stitch is to work to about eight stitches, then cut yarn, leaving 12" tail. Thread tail onto yarn needle and pull through remaining stitches firmly. Secure and weave in end. See gored toe on page 75.

## Greek or Zigzag Bind Off

This bind off is used on a top-down sock with a short-row toe. Be sure to start working the short rows on the bottom of the foot—the sole sts. The bind off will appear on the top of the sock—the instep stitches.

Arrange the stitches so that the stitches on the toe are closest to you and the working yarn is on the right end of the needles and comes from the stitches on the front needle.

**Set up:** P1 from the back needle and then K1 from the front needle. Pass the first stitch over the second stitch.

*P1 from the back needle, pass stitch on needle over, K1 from the front needle and pass stitch on needle over; rep from * across all stitches.

At end of work break off and draw tail through last loop to secure end.

Bind off

# BIND OFFS FOR TOE-UP SOCKS

Nothing is worse on a beautiful hand-knit sock than a bind off that is so tight you can't get the sock over your heel! Use one of these methods for a flexible bind off that will not only let you get your sock on, but will also help it keep its shape.

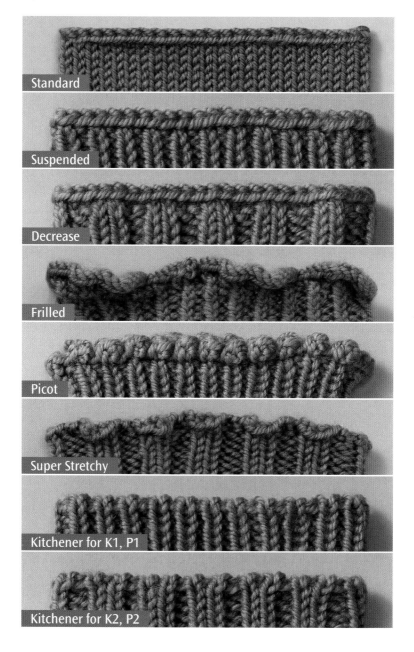

Standard

Suspended

Decrease

Frilled

Picot

Super Stretchy

Kitchener for K1, P1

Kitchener for K2, P2

## Standard Bind Off

Work two stitches in pattern, with the left-hand needle pull the first stitch over the second stitch and off the needle. *Work another stitch and pull the previous one over it. Repeat from * to end. Pull yarn through final loop to secure.

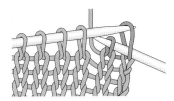

Pass first knitted stitch over
second stitch loosely.

## Suspended Bind Off

This method helps keep the stitches even on the bound-off edge so that they won't be too tight or prone to stretching in an uneven fashion. Work as for the standard bind off (above), but keep the lifted stitch on the left needle. Work the next stitch, as this stitch is retained on the point of the left-hand needle while the third or next stitch is knitted (fig. 1), when both the suspended stitch and new stitch are slipped off together in one movement. This will leave two stitches on the right-hand needle. Draw the first stitch over the second and retain it on the left-hand needle as before (fig. 2). Continue to end. Pull yarn through final loop to secure.

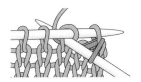

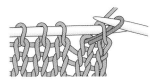

Fig. 1                         Fig. 2

## Decrease Bind Offs

There are three ways to work a decrease bind off. Versions 1 and 2 both produce a chain on the bound-off edge that looks like a standard bind off, but they vary in the way the stitches are worked together. Version 3 does not produce the chain across the top.

**Version 1:** Like the suspended bind off, this method produces an even bound-off edge. Knit the first stitch. *Slip the next stitch knitwise. Insert the left needle tip from left to right into the front of the two stitches on the right needle, and knit the two stitches together through the *back* loops. One stitch remains. Repeat from * to end. Pull yarn through final loop to secure.

**Version 2:** *Knit the first two stitches on the left-hand needle together through the back loops. Slip the stitch from the right-hand needle back to the left-hand needle. Repeat from * to end. Be careful not to pull too tight.

**Version 3:** This starts out the same as version 2, but knit the two stitches together through the *front* loops instead of the back loops. The end result is an edge that does not have the standard bind-off chain across the top, but it can be the perfect ending on the right sock.

## Frilled Bind Off

A frilled bind off doubles the number of stitches during the bind-off round, making a very loose, frilled edge. Use it with ribbing to make the bind off looser than the knitting. To bind off, work the first stitch, make one stitch by picking up the loop between the stitch on the left-hand and right-hand needles (M1), pass first stitch over the second stitch. *Work the next stitch on the left-hand needle, M1. Repeat from * to end. Pull yarn through final loop to secure.

The Sock Knitter's Handbook

## Picot Bind Off

To add elasticity to the bound-off edge without the picots being very visible: *Cast on one stitch using knitted cast on, bind off three stitches using the standard bind off (page 87), place the remaining stitch on the right-hand needle back on the left-hand needle as if to purl. Repeat from * to end. Pull yarn through final loop to secure.

## Super-Stretchy Bind Off

This bind off can be used for any toe-up sock; it's particularly useful for yarns with very little give such as linen, cotton, or blends of fibers that include little or no wool.

**Chain 1:** Start as for the basic knitted cast on (page 37), put right needle into first stitch on left needle, make a loop, bring it through, now drop the worked stitch off the left needle.

1. **(Set up):** K1, P1, past first stitch over second stitch. Chain 1.

2. K1, pass first stitch over the second.

3. P1, pass first stitch over the second.

4. Chain 1.

Repeat steps 2–4 around. Pull yarn through final loop to secure.

## Kitchener Bind Off for K1, P1 Ribbing

This bind off makes a very nice finished edge that's more attractive than a standard bind off.

Using two circular or double-pointed needles, depending on the number of stitches you have, separate the knit stitches from the purl stitches. As the stitches face you, (insert one needle into the first knit stitch, the second needle into the purl stitch) across. Half the stitches will be on one needle and half will be on the second needle. When you look at the knitting on either side, there will be knit stitches on the needle facing you (fig. 1).

Cut the working yarn about three times the width of the knitting plus about 12" extra to weave in. Thread yarn through a yarn needle. You'll direct the yarn needle as if it were a knitting needle, working the two pieces together on knitting needles held in the left hand. Graft the stitches together as follows:

1. Insert yarn needle through the first stitch on the front needle as if to purl. Leave stitch on needle. Insert yarn needle through first stitch on back needle as if to knit. Leave stitch on needle. Keep the yarn between the needles so it's not mistaken for another stitch (fig. 2). Adjust the tension as you work.

2. *Insert yarn needle through the first stitch on front needle as if to knit, and through next st on front needle as if to purl. Drop off first stitch on front needle.

3. Insert yarn needle through first stitch on back needle as if to purl, and through next st on back needle as if to knit. Drop off first stitch on back needle* (fig. 3). Repeat from * to * until there's one stitch on each needle.

4. Insert yarn needle through remaining stitch on front needle as if to knit and drop stitch off.

5. Insert yarn needle through remaining stitch on back needle as if to purl and drop stitch off. Finish by weaving in end.

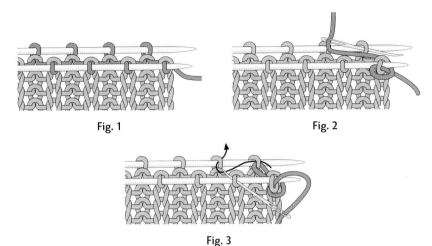

Fig. 1     Fig. 2

Fig. 3

## Kitchener Bind Off for K2, P2 Ribbing

You can modify the Kitchener bind off for K1, P1 ribbing to use for K2, P2 ribbing. Before you separate the stitches, knit the first knit stitch and place on the previous needle; this will be the last stitch grafted off. Start with a K1 on the front needle, then P2 on the back needle, then continue with K2 on the front, P2 on the back, and so on, ending with a K1. Work as for binding off K1, P1 ribbing.

# 🧶 Tips and Hints

Our combined years of experience knitting and designing socks has given us a wealth of knowledge—not only about sock knitting, but also about fixing socks and avoiding problems in the first place. You may have experienced one or two of these situations already and are in need of some help. Or if you're new to sock knitting, read ahead and learn about avoidable issues before you start your next pair of socks!

## REPAIRING SOCKS

Knitting a pair of socks takes time. Since socks often wear out at the heel or toe and these parts represent a small fraction of the total sock, frugal knitters from the past replaced the worn part(s) to save the sock and not have to knit a new pair. Since the knitter often did not have the exact same yarn, the new heel and/or toe were often done in a contrasting color. Knitters may have begun using contrasting colors for heels and toes to make it easier to remove and replace them. In the 1930s, a method of putting in a single row of contrasting-color yarn at the end of the heel turn was used to facilitate opening the heel.

To estimate how much yarn you'll need to replace the heel and/or the toe, weigh the sock. You'll need about 10% of the weight for the heel, and about 5% of the weight for the toe.

## Replacing a French Heel

Beth was taught to knit by her German paternal grandmother, "Oma," at the age of four. Here are Oma's instructions for replacing a French heel.

**Oma's Heel-Repair Instructions**
You'll need:

1 set of 5 double-pointed needles in same size originally used for sock

1 or 2 double-pointed needles, one or two sizes smaller

Yarn of a weight/color compatible with sock

Starting at the hole or at the bottom of the heel flap, unravel the heel flap and the heel turning. This is a little fussy, as you must cut the yarn or pull it through each time you ravel to the edge of the gusset.

You'll have two sets of "live" stitches: *At the top of heel flap/bottom of leg*, and **at end of heel turning/the round where the gusset stitches were picked up**. Pick up each set of stitches on a separate needle; use smaller needles if necessary but transfer to your "working" size.

Look at the stitch-like loops along the edge of the gussets where they were attached to the "old" heel flap. Put these loops on needles as if they were stitches; use smaller needles and transfer if necessary. The number of loops will be approximately one-half the number of the heel-flap stitches plus a few—there should be the same number on each side.

**Reknit the heel flap:** Start with the stitches at bottom of leg (* to * above), (slip 1, K1) across the heel flap stitches—if the number of stitches is odd, M1 near the center of the row in place of one K1. When you get to the end of the needle, knit the last stitch together with the first stitch on the gusset needle. Purl back and when you get to the last stitch, purl it together with the first stitch on the other gusset needle. Continue until all of the gusset stitches are used up and the heel flap is complete.

Turn the heel and graft using short rows. Knit across one-half the heel flap sts plus 2 sts.

**Row 1:** Ssk, K1. Turn. Sl 1, P5, P2tog, P1. Turn.

**Row 2:** Knit to 1 st before gap, ssk, K1. Turn.

**Row 3:** Purl to 1 st before gap, P2tog, P1. Turn.

Rep rows 2 and 3 until all edge sts are used. Graft the rem sts to the second set of live sts (** to ** above). As you graft, run your needle through the last gusset st at each side to prevent any gaps.

## Reknitting a Toe

If you wear out your toes on socks knit from the top down, you can simply cut off the toe, pick up the live stitches, and reknit a new toe. If the socks were knit from the toe up, you can still cut off the toe and knit a top-down style toe (page 74). Or you can knit your favorite toe-up toe (page 77) and graft it to the foot of the sock.

## START AT ANKLE AND WORK OUTWARD IN BOTH DIRECTIONS

Some people like to be sure to work ALL the yarn they have for their sock, especially if they've spun it themselves. Or, some people worry about working on a large sock and running out of yarn before it's finished. One option is to work a toe-up sock. If you're a dedicated top-down sock knitter, you have the option of using a provisional cast on in the middle of the sock and working in both directions. This way you've completed the foot with your yarn. You can then use what remains for the leg. The solution is that you get to knit a top-down sock and use up all the yarn.

Use a provisional cast on for the number of stitches for your sock. Work one round, and then begin the heel of your choice and finish the foot of the sock. Pick up the stitches from the provisional cast on—make sure you have the right amount. Then work the leg. Be careful about your choice of patterning. When you knit you have Vs for the knit stitches—you'll be off half a stitch when changing directions. It's OK if you have two rounds of reverse stockinette or some plain stockinette before ribbing continues; if you work ribbing immediately, there will be a noticeable jog at the place where you cast on.

## CUFF, TOE, AND HEEL IN CONTRASTING COLORS TO EXTEND SOCK YARN

If you're worried that you don't have enough yarn for a complete pair of socks, consider using another yarn for the cuff, heel, and toes. These three elements can use up to 20% of the yarn for the sock. This is a great way to extend the yarn while giving the sock a designed look, rather than ending up with the awkward-looking foot and toe in a different color.

## AVOIDING COLOR POOLS AND PATTERNS WITH HAND-PAINTED YARN

When hand-painted yarn forms patterns you don't want, it's usually because the circumference of the skein of painted yarn is some multiple of the length of the rounds of knitting in the sock. Here are some tricks that may help break up the color pools:

- Change the number of stitches
- Change the needle size
- Change the length of the knitted round. You can do this by incorporating slipped stitches, cables, or increases or decreases in the number of stitches worked in a round.

Some patterns we have found to work better with hand-painted yarn are: faceted rib (page 106), ric rac rib (page 107), baby cable rib (page 108), and slipped-stitch rib (page 114). A word of caution about slipped stitches: they may make a less elastic fabric, so if you choose this option, you may need more stitches or a larger needle size.

## CHANGING THE SIZE—BEYOND LOOKING AT NUMBER OF STITCHES

If you have a pattern for a sock that you think will not fit your foot, there are a number of ways to work with the pattern, yarn, or needles to produce a sock that will fit. The simplest solution is with a stockinette sock. The number of stitches is a formula of foot circumference and stitch gauge with needles and yarn. Changing the number of stitches in this case is the most straight-forward way to have a good sock that fits your foot. Most sock patterns are more complex than that. There may be a beautiful pattern included that is many stitches wide, the pattern is only written for one shoe size, or it's written for one particular yarn that you don't have or is no longer available. We have thought about these issues and offer you several options for changing the final size of the sock.

### Changing the Gauge by Changing the Needle Size

If you're uncertain that the sock pattern is going to fit to your satisfaction, first calculate the intended size. Divide the number of stitches by the stated gauge. Let's say the pattern is for a sock of 64 stitches and the gauge is 7½ stitches to the inch. That will give you a sock that is roughly 8½" in sock circumference. A swatch will let you know what changing needle size will do for your size and the kind of fabric you'll get by changing needle size. If you move to a much smaller needle size you may get a fabric that is too dense and harsh; conversely, if you change to a much larger needle size, it may result in fabric that is too loose and will wear out very rapidly.

"Fingering"-weight or "sock"-weight yarn covers a wide range of yards per 100 gram ball of yarn. If you're trying to make a larger sock, try picking a heavier yarn—this will knit happily on needles in the larger part of the range and yield a larger sock. If, however, you need to make a smaller sock, consider a yarn with more yardage (a thinner yarn) that you can knit with smaller needles and have a sock that fits better.

The yardage of a 100-gram skein varies from 310 yards to 480 yards. Remembering that the lesser-yardage yarn will be somewhat thicker, choose a yarn with fewer yards to produce a dense, wearable fabric. You can also take this option in the other direction. By combining a thinner fingering-weight yarn with the smaller needles, you can avoid a sock fabric that is too dense or too hard to work on.

## Changing the Gauge by Changing the Yarn Weight

When a pattern is a women's Medium (size 8 or 8½ shoe), it can be a pretty easy change to a woman's Extra Large. Most patterns are written for fingering-weight yarn at about 7½ stitches per inch. The same pattern knit in sport-weight yarn on size 3 needles gives a gauge of 6½ stitches per inch, which is almost exactly the 10" sock circumference needed.

Let's review the math. The original pattern had 64 stitches at a gauge of 7½ stitches per inch; 64 stitches divided by stitches per inch equals an 8½" sock circumference. With a wee bit of ease, this sock will fit shoe size 8 (8⅜" sock circumference) or shoe size 8½ (8½" sock circumference).

If we knit the same 64 stitches at sport-weight gauge of 6½ stitches per inch, the 64 stitches divided by 6½ stitches per inch equals 9⅞", which, with a wee bit of ease, brings us right up to the required 10" sock circumference.

First, look at the typical knit gauges for each weight of yarn and calculate the conversion. Remember that for good wear, socks are typically knit on smaller needles than those indicated on the ball band. Second, swatch the yarn you intend to use with several different needle sizes. Check your swatches to see which one achieved the gauge you require and a fabric dense enough to wear well. Finally, knit with the new yarn and needles and enjoy the pattern you converted.

## Changing the Number of Pattern Repeats

The next option for changing sock size is to resize the pattern. If the pattern has a moderate repeat no more than six or eight stitches, this is likely the best way to go. Changing the size most frequently means adding or subtracting two pattern repeats, so you do not have to split the stitches of a single repeat between the instep and the heel. If it's not possible to add or subtract two repeats, you can make up for the half repeat with several stockinette stitches at each side of the instep.

Working out the math for a smaller or larger sock can be challenging, but you really don't need to do it if you use a sock calculator. Several are available online. Our favorite is Mary Moran's Sockcalc, available as a download from her website for your personal use at:

http://www.knittingzone.com/mysocks.htm

Others we're aware of are:

www.panix.com/~ilaine/socks.html

www.princeton.edu/~ezb/sockform.html

If you're likely to modify sock sizes frequently and want a variety of options including knitting from the top down, knitting from the toe up, choosing your own heels, and so on, consider an investment in sock-knitting software. Mary Moran's is called "The Sole Solution," and Carole Wulster's is called "Sock Wizard." They're available from their respective websites and are also sold at many yarn shops.

For an extensive collection of socks designed using the technique of changing the number of pattern repeats, see *Sensational Knitted Socks* (Martingale & Company, 2005) and *More Sensational Knitted Socks* (Martingale & Company, 2007), both by Charlene Schurch.

## Changing the Spacing (Number of Stitches) between Pattern Elements

Often a sock design has one or more prominent elements, such as cables, around the leg of the sock. These elements are usually separated by two or more knit stitches or purl stitches. Let's use the example of a 64-stitch sock that has a pattern bit of six stitches with two purl stitches between. The sock has eight pattern repeats. If we want a smaller sock and work only one purl stitch between the six stitches, the pattern will be seven stitches, yielding a 56-stitch sock. If we are working at 8 stitches per inch, we have just subtracted one inch of sock, which will perhaps make the sock fit perfectly. If you need to make the sock larger, you can add a purl stitch or two to the between-the-pattern part. Each time you add a purl stitch, you've added an inch. This makes it much simpler to maintain the sock's look without a lot of redesign.

## Changing the Number of Background Stitches around a Centered Motif

In some socks, a cable or centered motif is centered on the front or back of the sock, and the remainder of the sock is worked in stockinette stitch or ribbing. Within limits, increasing or decreasing the amount of stockinette stitch or ribbing to the required number of stitches for the size desired should be relatively simple. Two important considerations should apply. First, the gauge of the motif is likely different from the gauge of the stockinette stitch or ribbing. Starting with the stated sock circumference, add or subtract stitches based on the gauge of stockinette stitch or ribbing to achieve the desired measurement. Second, the sock size must not be decreased to the point that the motif becomes more than half of the total stitches. This would create a problem when dividing the stitches for the heel and instep.

## Changing Elements within a Repeat

Some pattern repeats seem large—they could be 20 stitches or more—but if you look carefully the pattern is a combination of several narrower elements. If you need to change the number of stitches for a well-fitting sock, first consider how many repeats there are in the sock, that is, are there four or six pattern repeats around the leg? Next you need to decide how many stitches you need to change for the total number to fit the intended foot. For this example, if we have six repeats of the complex pattern, we need to add 12 stitches to make the sock fit. We need to look at the pattern repeat and add two stitches to each repeat. This could involve adding ribbing or extending part of a pattern, or is there a little bit of seed stitch? Can you make a cable two stitches wider? The same thing would apply if you need fewer stitches for your selected pattern. Can you subtract from some ribbing or a stockinette stripe, or make a cable two stitches narrower?

## Adding a Small Motif between Pattern Repeats

Some socks are designed with a complex pattern that is half the sock and is just too beautiful not to knit—but it isn't the right size, and changing the needle size or yarn is not an option. Try looking at the chart and see if you can add the needed stitches in a different, related pattern that will clearly be a complementary design element. If this one large pattern is too big, consider taking a few stitches from each side, checking carefully to make sure the join is the same on both sides and looks like it was intended. The opportunities to apply this device to other situations seem almost unlimited.

## SPECIAL FIT ISSUES

As mentioned earlier, not all feet look exactly alike. From short toes to thin ankles to a high instep, you'll find ways to customize the fit of your socks in this section.

## High Instep

The easiest way to provide for more sock fabric for a high instep is to use a French heel worked from the top down. Measure your heel and determine how many more rows you need for a heel flap, then work the longer heel flap. Work the rest of the French heel as described in the French heel instructions on page 54, but you'll be picking up more stitches along the heel flap, and the gusset decrease sections will be longer than the original. You also have the option of working two plain rounds for each decrease round for the gusset to provide for a longer and roomier gusset.

If you're working a Strong heel, you may add additional rounds but not additional increases to the patterning to accommodate a higher instep. A typical French heel has four more rows than the typical Strong heel.

## Thin Ankles

This is the case where your ankles are thinner than the ball of your foot. Make sure you use a stretchy rib pattern on the leg of your socks, as this will allow your foot to travel through the leg when you're putting the socks on, and it will help the sock hug the leg and ankle rather than slouching down.

## Thick Ankles

When your ankles are wider than the ball of your foot, you may have a problem with the foot of your sock feeling big and sloppy. Consider making the foot smaller and using smaller needles for the foot to make the gauge denser. Another option is to use a stretchy rib on the instep of the foot, which will add elasticity to the sock.

## Wide Ball of the Foot with Narrow Heel

The sock for this situation needs to be wide enough for the ball of the foot yet stretchy enough to feel snug when worn and not sag. Knit the leg and instep in a stretchy rib; you may want to use 40% of the stitches of the sock for the heel so that it's not too large for the narrow heel.

## Wide Heels

If you have trouble having enough sock for your heel to fit comfortably, use between 60% and 66% of the stitches of the sock to knit the heel. This will make the socks easier to put on as well as more comfortable to wear.

## Narrow Heels

If heels tend to be too wide when using the standard 50% formula, consider using 40% to 45% of the stitches for the heel and the remainder for the instep. Even though you have fewer stitches in the heel, make sure to make the heel long enough by using a measurement rather than a stitch count. A stretchy ribbed pattern on the leg and instep will help pull in any extra fabric that may result from the change in proportion. If you have very narrow feet as well, you may want to also decrease stitches on the instep, or use smaller needles to create a smaller foot and heel area.

## AVOIDING A TIGHT CAST ON

The cast-on edge of a sock does not need to be as durable as, say, the cuff edge of a sweater. But it must be elastic enough for the heel of the wearer to pass through as well as loose enough so as not to leave marks on the wearer's calf.

To make sure you have a loose cast on, we have two suggestions. One is to use the frilled cast on (page 34). The other suggestion is to use the cast on of your choosing, but be careful to leave some space between the stitches you're casting on. The looseness of a cast on is in the yarn between the stitches, not in the stitch. Ensuring you have some distance between the stitches will make the yarn between longer and looser.

## AVOIDING A GAP AT TOP OF GUSSET

The hole or gap at the top of the gusset is a perennial problem for sock knitters. Some instructions don't provide any suggestion for how to alleviate this situation, while some suggest picking up one stitch, without any specifics on exactly where or how to do this.

We like to pick up two extra stitches at the top of the gusset. The way to identify these stitches is to look for the horizontal thread between the first instep stitch and the heel-flap stitch. Insert the needle into the left half of the heel-flap stitch and pick up one stitch; then pick up the right half of the first instep stitch from the row below the stitch on the needle. Both of these stitches are on the gusset needle. If you're having trouble identifying where to pick up the stitches, insert a double-pointed needle following the horizontal thread connecting the stitches; you're looking for the center between the two halves of the two stitches.

When picking up the gusset on the other side of the sock, again locate the horizontal thread between the instep and heel flap; pick up the outside halves of each stitch and place them on the needle to be used for the heel gusset. If these stitches have been purled, just pick up through the purl bump (fig. 2). These two extra stitches are worked together on the first gusset round.

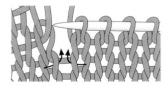

**Fig. 1**
Picking up stitches
when both were knit

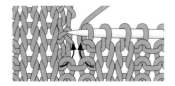

**Fig. 2**
Picking up stitches
when both were purled

## AVOIDING EARS OR HOLES ON HEEL TURNS

As careful as we were about picking up stitches for the gusset, we would sometimes notice a little ear at one side of the heel turn. In thinking about the way most socks are knit, we realized that there's one extra row worked after the heel is turned. If you're working with heavier yarn, this extra row would account for the ear. So we tried completing the heel turn on a right-side row, eliminating the need to work a plain knit row before picking up gusset stitches. And that eliminated the ear! This way of working is not standard, and for those of you who reflexively knit that way, pay attention to the instructions; all the heel flaps start on a wrong-side row, because you turn first, not after the first row has been worked.

Look at the heel flap as you begin to pick up stitches. It's counterintuitive, but not picking up the very first stitch at the bottom will make a smoother heel as well as eliminate the chance for a hole. It seems like an extra stitch picked up would lessen the chance of a hole—but that hasn't been our experience. Try not picking up the very first stitch and see how you like the result.

## AVOIDING EARS ON GRAFTED TOES

The stitches that are worked last as you work the grafting of the toe may become stretched slightly. As you finish working them they may seem larger than the ones in the middle. To avoid this, work the Kitchener grafting rather tightly. When finished grafting, thread the yarn on the tapestry needle into the space between the last two stitches grafted together. Then weave in the yarn end on the inside of the sock. You can tighten the last stitch a bit to make sure that last end does not stick up.

## AVOIDING A JOG AT CAST-ON/BIND-OFF EDGE

One way to even the cast-on round is to take the tail from the cast on and work it between the first and last stitches to even them out. Another alternative is to cast on one extra stitch. As you're working the first round, work the first stitch and the last stitch together as follows: Slip the last stitch, work the first (first stitch or round 2), and pass the last stitch over the first.

# GETTING THE MOST MILEAGE FROM YOUR SOCKS

| PLACE OF WEAR | SOCK DIRECTION | HELPFUL SUGGESTIONS | POOR ALTERNATIVES |
|---|---|---|---|
| Back of Heel | Top down: Any of the heel-flap socks (French, Dutch or shaped common) | • Use heel stitch or eye of partridge st (page 56)<br>• Add reinforcing yarn when working heel flap | Short-row heel or any heel with stockinette worked at back of heel. |
| | Toe up: Reverse French heel | • Use heel stitch or eye of partridge st (page 56)<br>• Add reinforcing yarn when working heel flap | |
| Pad of Heel | Top down: French heel | • Use reinforcing yarn when working heel turn.<br>• Continue heel stitch on the heel turn and gusset for denser fabric | Avoid unreinforced stockinette here |
| | Top down: Strong heel | • This heel has the largest heel turn, add reinforcing or use a smaller needle size | |
| | Top down: either French or Strong heel | • Add a row of waste yarn after the last heel turn row. You can then unpick this and pull out to reknit this section. | |
| | Toe up: Work top-down French heel | • Work the heel flap on the bottom of the foot and use heel stitch or reinforcing yarn. | |

| | | |
|---|---|---|
| Toe | Top down | • Use a smaller needle size from the one used for the foot; this may shorten the toe, so measure.<br>• Use reinforcing yarn.<br>• Easy to cut worn toe off and reknit it. | Using too small a needle will create an easily worn-out toe. |
| | Toe up | • Use smaller needle and make sure toe is long enough.<br>• To reknit, cut worn torn and reknit a standard toe. | |
| Ball of foot | Both | • Use a smaller needle for the bottom of the foot.<br>• Knit the portion of the bottom of the foot with the heel stitch; be aware that it's narrower and denser than stockinette. | Avoid loose-gauge stockinette. |

## ADDING NEW YARN

Most of the time the skeins of yarn will be enough to knit one sock. However, if you're using leftovers, knitting stripes, or you've run out and are adding new yarn, this method works well for socks, as for most other knitting projects. Stop knitting when there's a tail of at least 4", and then lay the new yarn alongside the old yarn and knit the next two stitches with both yarns held together. Be sure to leave a 4" tail on the new yarn. Drop the old yarn and continue with the new yarn. After you knit past this addition, tighten stitches by pulling on the tails. Even with very fine or bulky yarn, tugging on the tails will make a thick spot in the knitting. When you're finished, use a darning needle and weave in both ends. This is secure, and the stitches will not work themselves out.

## WORKING WITH MULTIPLE COLORS

Patterns worked with multiple colors, such as Fair Isle and mosaic, are less elastic than plain patterns knit with one color. It may make a better sock if you work the leg with a larger needle, which will make the leg a little larger and easier to get your heel into the foot of the sock. This is also true when working slipped-stitch patterns, one color or two.

## IMPROVING DURABILITY

Generally, knitting more densely will help with the wearability of your socks. Do a gauge swatch and make sure you have a good, dense fabric that when held to the light doesn't look open or lacy. These suggestions are based on the knitter's ability to work a denser fabric without drastically changing the size and shape of the sock.

## WORKING A TOP-DOWN HEEL ON A TOE-UP SOCK

The structure of a heel is to make a sharp turn in the tube that is the sock. If you need additional durability on the pad of the heel, consider working a toe-up sock but work the French heel instructions for top down (page 54). This will place the heel flap on the pad of the heel. Any heel can be worked on any sock—it may look different, but think about the advantages the parts of the heel offer and place it where you like.

# 🧶 Stitch Dictionary

The charts for the stitch patterns represent what the knitting looks like from the right side, or outside, of the work and are for working the pattern in the round only. All charts are read from right to left for every round and from bottom to top.

In some patterns, the written directions begin with a stitch [indicated in brackets] and the charts begin with a separate column. This extra stitch is worked only once at the beginning of the round of the instep. When working the leg, work only the stitch repeats, not the extra stitch. The extra stitch balances the total pattern on the instep.

| | | | |
|---|---|---|---|
| K | | sl 1-K2tog-psso | |
| P | | sl 1-K2-psso | |
| K1b | | K3 and pass first st over next 2 sts | |
| No stitch | | Knit into back of second st on needle and leave st on needle, knit first st and sl both sts off needle | |
| sl 1 wyib | | | |
| sl 1 wyif | | | |
| YO | | Knit into front of second st on needle and leave st on needle, knit first st and sl both sts off needle | |
| M1L | | | |
| M1R | | | |
| K1, YO, K1 in same st | | K2tog and leave st on needle, knit first st and sl both sts off needle | |
| K1, P1, K1 in front of same st | | | |
| Purl into front of st and keep on needle, knit into back of st, sl both sts off needle | | Sl 2 sts to cn, hold in back, K1, K2 from cn | |
| ssk | | Sl 1 st to cn, hold in front, K2, K1 from cn | |
| K2tog | | | |
| P2tog | | Sl 3 sts to cn and hold in front, K3, K3 from cn | |
| P3tog | | | |
| P3tog, knit same 3 sts tog, purl same 3 sts tog again, and sl all 3 sts from needle | | BO | |

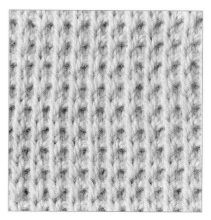

## Roman Rib Stitch
(Multiple of 2 sts)

**Rnds 1, 2, 5, and 6:** Knit.

**Rnds 3 and 4:** *K1, P1; rep from *.

**Rnd 7 and 8:** *P1, K1; rep from *.

Rep rnds 1–8.

## Faceted Rib
(Multiple of 2 sts)

**Rnds 1 and 2:** [K1], knit.

**Rnd 3:** [K1], *sl 1, K1; rep from *.

**Rnd 4:** [P1], *sl 1, P1; rep from *.

Rep rnds 1–4.

The Sock Knitter's Handbook

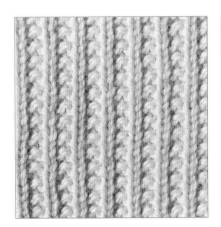

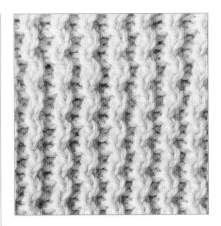

## Farrow Rib
**(Multiple of 3 sts)**

**Rnd 1:** *K2, P1; rep from *.

**Rnd 2:** *K1, P2; rep from *.

Rep rnds 1 and 2.

## Ric Rac Rib
**(Multiple of 3 sts)**

**Rnds 1 and 3:** [P1] *K2, P1; rep from *.

**Rnd 2:** [P1] *Knit into front of second st on needle and leave st on needle, knit first st and sl both sts off needle.

**Rnd 4:** [P1] *Knit into back of second st on needle and leave st on needle, knit first st and sl both sts off needle.

P1; rep from *.

Rep rnds 1–4.

## Garter Rib
**(Multiple of 4 sts)**

**Rnd 1:** *K2, P2; rep from *.

**Rnd 2:** Knit.

Rep rnds 1 and 2.

## Baby Cable Rib
**(Multiple of 4 sts)**

**Rnds 1, 2, and 3:** *K2, P2; rep from *.

**Rnd 4:** *K2tog and leave st on needle, knit first st and sl both sts off needle, P2; rep from *.

Rep rnds 1–4.

## Seeded Rib
**(Multiple of 4 sts)**

**Rnd 1:** [K1], *K1, P1, K2; rep from *.

**Rnd 2:** [K1], *P3, K1; rep from *.

Rep rnds 1 and 2.

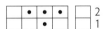

## Stansfield 12
**(Multiple of 4 sts)**

**Rnds 1 and 2:** [P1], *K1, P3; rep from *.

**Rnds 3 and 4:** [P1], *K1, P1, K1, P1; rep from *.

**Rnds 5 and 6:** [P1], *P2, K1, P1; rep from *.

**Rnds 7 and 8:** [P1], *K1, P1, K1, P1; rep from *.

Rep rnds 1–8.

## Seed-Stitch Rib
**(Multiple of 4 sts)**

**Rnd 1:** [K1], *P1, K1, P1, K1; rep from *.

**Rnd 2:** [K1], *P3, K1; rep from *.

Rep rnds 1 and 2.

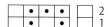

## Yarn over Cable
**(Multiple of 5 sts)**

**Rnd 1:** *P1, sl 1-K2-psso, P1; rep from *.

**Rnd 2:** *P1, K1, YO, K1, P1; rep from *.

**Rnds 3 and 4:** *P1, K3, P1; rep from *.

Rep rnds 1–4 .

The Sock Knitter's Handbook

## Beaded Rib
**(Multiple of 5 sts)**

**Rnd 1:** *P1, K1, P1, K1, P1; rep from *.

**Rnd 2:** *P1, K3, P1; rep from *.

Rep rnds 1 and 2.

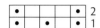

## Little Shell Rib
**(Multiple of 5 sts)**

**Rnds 1 and 2:** *P1, K3, P1; rep from *.

**Rnd 3:** *P1, sl 1-K2tog-psso, P1; rep from *.

**Rnd 4:** *P1, (K1, P1, K1) in front of next st, P1; rep from *.

Rep rnds 1–4.

## Willow Buds
(Multiple of 5 sts)

**Rnds 1 and 3:** *P1, K3, P1; rep from *.

**Rnd 2:** *P1, P3tog, knit same 3 sts tog, purl same 3 sts tog again, and sl all 3 sts from needle, P1; rep from *.

**Rnd 4:** *P1, K3, P1; rep from *.

Rep rnds 1–4 .

## Sailor's Rib
(Multiple of 5 sts)

**Rnd 1:** [K1b], *P1, K2, P1, K1b; rep from *.

**Rnd 2:** [K1], *P1, K2, P1, K1; rep from *.

**Rnd 3:** [K1b], *P4, K1b; rep from *.

**Rnd 4:** [K1], *P4, K1; rep from *.

Rep rnds 1–4.

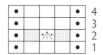

## Open Twisted Rib
(Multiple of 5 sts)

**Rnd 1:** [K1b], *P1, K2, P1, K1b; rep from *.

**Rnd 2:** [K1b], *P1, K1, YO, K1, P1, K1b; rep from *.

**Rnd 3:** [K1b], *P1, K3, P1, K1b; rep from *.

**Rnd 4:** [K1b], *P1, K3, pass first st over next 2 sts, P1, K1b; rep from *.

Rep rnds 1–4.

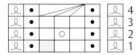

## Twin Rib
(Multiple of 6 sts)

**Rnd 1:** *K3, P3; rep from *.

**Rnd 2:** *K1, P1; rep from *.

Rep rnds 1 and 2.

## Slipped-Stitch Rib
(Multiple of 6 sts)

**Rnd 1:** *K3, P3; rep from *.

**Rnd 2:** *K1, sl 1 wyib, K1, P1, sl 1 wyif, P1; rep from *.

Rep rnds 1 and 2.

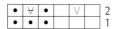

## Stansfield #10
(Multiple of 6 sts)

**Rnd 1:** *K3, P3; rep from *.

**Rnd 2:** *K3, P1, K1, P1; rep from *.

**Rnd 3:** *P4, K1, P1; rep from *.

**Rnd 4:** *K3, P1, K1, P1; rep from *.

Rep rnds 1–4.

The Sock Knitter's Handbook

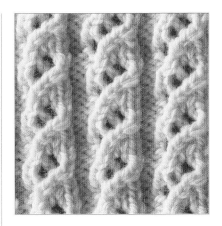

## Cloverleaf Eyelet Cable
(Multiple of 6 sts)

**Rnds 1, 3, and 5:** *K3, P3; rep from *.

**Rnd 2:** *YO, sl 1-K2tog-psso, YO, P3; rep from *.

**Rnd 4:** *K1, YO, ssk, P3; rep from *.

**Rnd 6:** *K3, P3; rep from *.

Rep rnds 1–6 .

## Waterfall Rib
(Multiple of 6 sts)

**Rnd 1:** *K3, P3; rep from *.

**Rnd 2:** *K3, YO, P3; rep from *.

**Rnd 3:** *K4, P3; rep from *.

**Rnd 4:** *K1, K2tog, YO, K1, P3; rep from *.

**Rnd 5:** *K2tog, K2, P3; rep from *.

**Rnd 6:** *K1, YO, K2tog, P3; rep from *.

Rep rnds 1–6.

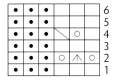

## Crosshatch Lace
(Multiple of 6 sts)

**Rnd 1:** *K3, K2tog, YO, K1; rep from *.

**Rnd 2:** *K2, K2tog, YO, K2; rep from *.

**Rnd 3:** *K1, K2tog, YO, K3; rep from *.

**Rnd 4:** *K2tog, YO, K4; rep from *.

**Rnd 5:** *K1, YO, ssk, K3; rep from *.

**Rnd 6:** *K2, YO, ssk, K2; rep from *.

**Rnd 7:** *K3, YO, ssk, K1; rep from *.

**Rnd 8:** *K4, YO, ssk; rep from *.

Rep rnds 1–8.

## Broad Spiral Rib
(Multiple of 6 sts)

**Rnds 1 and 3:** *P1, K4, P1; rep from *.

**Rnd 2:** *P1, (K2tog and leave st on needle, knit first st and sl both sts off needle) 2 times, P1; rep from * 2 times, P1; rep from *.

**Rnd 4:** *P1, K1, K2tog and leave st on needle, knit first st and sl both sts off needle, K1, P1; rep from *.

Rep rnds 1–4.

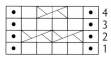

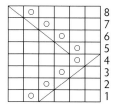

The Sock Knitter's Handbook

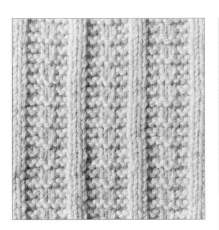

## Shadow Rib
(Multiple of 8 sts)

**Rnds 1 and 3:** Knit.

**Rnd 2:** *K1, P6, K1; rep from *.

**Rnd 4:** *K1, P2, K2, P2, K1; rep from *.

Rep rnds 1–4.

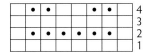

## Slipped-Stitch Cable
(Multiple of 8 sts)

**Rnd 1:** *K6, P2; rep from *.

**Rnds 2–5:** *Sl 1 wyif, K4, sl 1 wyif, P2; rep from *.

**Rnd 6:** *Sl 1 st to cn, hold in front, K2, K1 from cn, sl 2 sts to cn, hold in back, K1, K2 from cn, P2; rep from *.

Rep rnds 1–6.

## Scrolls
(Multiple of 8 sts)

**Rnd 1:** *YO, K6, K2tog; rep from *.

**Rnd 2:** *K1, YO, K5, K2tog; rep from *.

**Rnd 3:** *K2, YO, K4, K2tog; rep from *.

**Rnd 4:** *K3, YO, K3, K2tog; rep from *.

**Rnd 5:** *K4, YO, K2, K2tog; rep from *.

**Rnd 6:** *K5, YO, K1, K2tog; rep from *.

**Rnd 7:** *K6, YO, K2tog; rep from *.

**Rnd 8:** *Ssk, K6, YO; rep from *.

**Rnd 9:** *Ssk, K5, YO, K1; rep from *.

**Rnd 10:** *Ssk, K4, YO, K2; rep from *.

**Rnd 11:** *Ssk, K3, YO, K3; rep from *.

**Rnd 12:** *Ssk, K2, YO, K4; rep from *.

**Rnd 13:** *Ssk, K1, YO, K5; rep from *.

**Rnd 14:** *Ssk, YO, K6; rep from *.

Rep rnds 1–14.

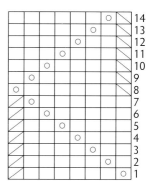

The Sock Knitter's Handbook

## 3 x 3 Cable with Moss Stitch
(Multiple of 11 sts)

**Rnds 1, 2, 5, and 6:** *P1, K1, P1, K1, P1, K6; rep from *.

**Rnds 3 and 4:** *P2, K1, P2, K6; rep from *.

**Rnd 7:** *P2, K1, P2, sl 3 sts to cn and hold in front, K3, K3 from cn; rep from *.

**Rnd 8:** *P2, K1, P2, K6; rep from *.

Rep rnds 1–8.

## Ridged Feather
(Multiple of 11 sts)

**Rnds 1 and 2:** Knit.

**Rnd 3:** *P2tog twice, YO, (K1, YO) 3 times, P2tog twice; rep from *.

**Rnd 4:** Knit.

Rep rnds 1–4.

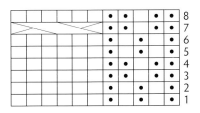

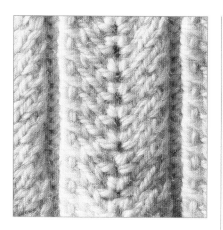

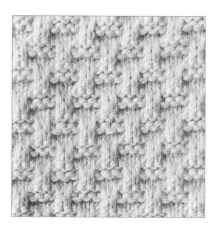

## Chevron
(Multiple of 11 sts)

**Rnd 1:** *P2, K2tog, K2, (K1, YO, K1) in next st, K2, ssk; rep from *.

**Rnd 2:** *P2, K9; rep from *.

Rep rnds 1 and 2.

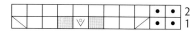

## Basket Check
(Multiple of 12 sts)

Sl all sts wyif.

**Rnds 1, 2, 7, and 8:** Knit.

**Rnds 3 and 5:** *Sl 1, K4, sl 2, K4, sl 1; rep from *.

**Rnds 4 and 6:** *Sl 1, P4, sl 2, P4, sl 1; rep from *.

**Rnds 9 and 11:** *K2, sl 2, K4, sl 2, K2; rep from *.

**Rnds 10 and 12:** *P2, sl 2, P4, sl 2, P2; rep from *.

Rep rnds 1–12.

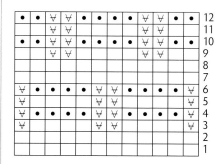

# Abbreviations & Glossary

**approx** approximately

**beg** beginning

**BO** bind off

**cn** cable needle

**CO** cast on

**cont** continue(s)

**dec(s)** decrease(s), decreasing

**dpn(s)** double-pointed needle(s)

**EOR** every other row

**g** gram

**inc(s)** increase(s), increasing

**K** knit

**KCGS** knit close gap stitch (page 70)

**K1b** knit 1 stitch through back loop

**K2tog** knit 2 stitches together—1 stitch decreased

**kw** knitwise

**LH** left hand

**m** meter

**mm** millimeter

**M1L** make 1 stitch that slants to the left—1 stitch increased

**M1R** make 1 stitch that slants to the right—1 stitch increased

**MC** main color

**oz** ounces

**P** purl

**P2tog** purl 2 stitches together—1 stitch decreased

**P3tog** purl 3 stitches together—2 stitches decreased

**PCGS** purl close gap stitch (page 70)

**PM** place marker

**psso** pass slipped stitch over

**PU** pick up and knit

**pw** purlwise

**rem** remain, remaining

**rep(s)** repeat(s)

**RH** right hand

**RS** right side

**sl** slip

**sl 1-K2-psso** slip 1 stitch knitwise, knit 2 stitches, pass slipped stitch over—1 stitch decreased

**sl 1-K2tog-psso** slip 1 stitch knitwise, knit 2 stitches together, pass slipped stitch over the knit 2 together—2 stitches decreased

**sl 1** slip 1 stitch purlwise with yarn in back unless otherwise noted

**ssk** slip 2 stitches knitwise, one at a time, to right needle, then insert left needle from left to right into front loops and knit 2 stitches together—1 stitch decreased

**st(s)** stitch(es)

**St st** stockinette stitch

**tog** together

**wyib** with yarn in back

**wyif** with yarn in front

**WS** wrong side

**yb** yarn back

**yds** yards

**yf** yarn forward

**YO** yarn over

# Stitches & Repeats Chart

| Stitches in Foot | Stitches in Pattern Repeat | | | | | | | | | | |
|---|---|---|---|---|---|---|---|---|---|---|---|
| | 2 | 3 | 4 | 5 | 6 | 7 | 8 | 9 | 10 | 11 | 12 |
| 28 | | | | | | X | | | | | |
| 30 | | X | | X | | | | | | | |
| 32 | X | | X | | | | X | | | | |
| 36 | X | X | | | X | | | X | | | |
| 40 | X | X | | X | | | | | X | | |
| 42 | | X | | | | X | | | | | |
| 44 | X | | | | | | | | | X | |
| 48 | X | X | X | | X | | X | | | | X |
| 50 | | | X | | | | | | | | |
| 52 | X | | | | | | | | | | |
| 54 | | X | | | | | | X | | | |
| 56 | X | | X | | | X | | | | | |
| 60 | X | X | | X | X | | | | X | | |
| 64 | X | | X | | | | X | | | | |
| 66 | | X | | | | | | | | X | |
| 68 | X | | | | | | | | | | |
| 70 | | | | X | | X | | | | | |
| 72 | X | X | X | | X | | | X | | | X |
| 76 | X | | | | | | | | | | |
| 78 | | X | | | | | | | | | |
| 80 | X | | X | X | | | X | | X | | |
| 84 | X | X | | | X | X | | | | | |
| 88 | X | | X | | | | | | | X | |
| 90 | | X | | X | | | | | | | |
| 92 | X | | | | | | | | | | |
| 96 | X | X | X | | X | | X | | | | X |
| 98 | | | | | | X | | | | | |

**Note:** Some stitch counts aren't marked in the chart, because when divided for instep and heel, the number of stitches on the instep won't be sufficient to work full pattern repeats. For example, a 44-stitch sock knit in a 4-stitch pattern, will yield 11 full repeats on the leg. But when dividing stitches evenly, you'll have 22 stitches for the instep—enough for just 5½ repeats. You can divide the stitches unevenly (20 and 24) to make 5 pattern repeats on the instep. Or work a plain pattern on the instep.

# Foot Measurements & Shoe Sizes

You'll find it helpful to know the foot circumference, the length of the foot, the height of the leg you want to knit, and the height of the heel. If the socks are for you, it's easy to measure your bare foot. If you cannot measure the recipient's foot, refer to the charts provided here for children, women, and men based on shoe size.

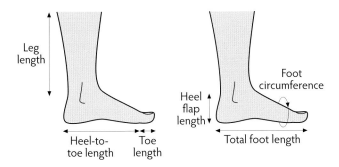

| Size Chart for Children | | | | | | |
|---|---|---|---|---|---|---|
| SHOE SIZE | FOOT CIRCUMFERENCE IN INCHES | SOCK LENGTH IN INCHES | | | | |
| | | Leg | Heel Flap | Heel to Toe | Toe | Total Foot Length |
| 4 | 5 | 2⅞ | 1⅜ | 3⅜ | ⅞ | 4¼ |
| 5 | 5¼ | 3¼ | 1⅜ | 3½ | 1¼ | 4¾ |
| 6 | 5½ | 3¼ | 1¾ | 3¾ | 1¼ | 5 |
| 7 | 5¾ | 3⅝ | 1¾ | 4 | 1¼ | 5¼ |
| 8 | 6¼ | 3¾ | 1⅞ | 4¾ | 1¼ | 5½ |
| 9 | 6¼ | 4⅛ | 1⅞ | 4¾ | 1¼ | 6 |
| 10 | 6¾ | 4⅜ | 1⅞ | 4¾ | 1½ | 6¼ |
| 11 | 6¾ | 4¾ | 2 | 5⅛ | 1⅝ | 6¾ |
| 12 | 6¾ | 5 | 2 | 5⅜ | 1⅝ | 7 |
| 13 | 7 | 5¼ | 2 | 5¾ | 1⅝ | 7⅜ |

# Size Chart for Women

| SHOE SIZE | FOOT CIRCUMFERENCE IN INCHES | | | SOCK LENGTH IN INCHES | | | | |
|---|---|---|---|---|---|---|---|---|
| | Narrow | Medium | Wide | Leg | Heel Flap | Heel to Toe | Toe | Total Foot Length |
| 5 | 6⅝ | 7½ | 8⅜ | 6⅛ | 2 | 7⅛ | 1⅝ | 8¾ |
| 5½ | 6¾ | 7⅝ | 8½ | 6¼ | 2 | 7¼ | 1⅝ | 8⅞ |
| 6 | 6⅞ | 7¾ | 8¾ | 6¼ | 2⅛ | 7¼ | 1¾ | 9 |
| 6½ | 7⅛ | 7⅞ | 8¾ | 6½ | 2⅛ | 7½ | 1¾ | 9¼ |
| 7 | 7¼ | 8⅛ | 9 | 6½ | 2¼ | 7⅝ | 1¾ | 9⅜ |
| 7½ | 7¼ | 8¼ | 9⅛ | 6¾ | 2¼ | 7¾ | 1¾ | 9½ |
| 8 | 7½ | 8⅜ | 9¼ | 6¾ | 2¼ | 8 | 1¾ | 9¾ |
| 8½ | 7⅝ | 8½ | 9⅜ | 6⅞ | 2¼ | 8 | 1¾ | 9¾ |
| 9 | 7¾ | 8¾ | 9½ | 7 | 2¼ | 8 | 2 | 10 |
| 9½ | 7⅞ | 8¾ | 9¾ | 7¼ | 2¼ | 8¼ | 2 | 10¼ |
| 10 | 8⅛ | 9 | 9¾ | 7¼ | 2¼ | 8¼ | 2 | 10¼ |
| 10½ | 8¼ | 9⅛ | 10 | 7⅜ | 2⅜ | 8½ | 2 | 10½ |
| 11 | 8⅜ | 9¼ | 10⅛ | 7⅝ | 2⅜ | 8¾ | 2 | 10¾ |
| 11½ | 8½ | 9⅜ | 10¼ | 7¾ | 2⅜ | 8¾ | 2 | 10¾ |
| 12 | 8¾ | 9½ | 10⅜ | 7⅞ | 2⅜ | 9 | 2 | 11 |

# Size Chart for Men

| SHOE SIZE | FOOT CIRCUMFERENCE IN INCHES | | | SOCK LENGTH IN INCHES | | | | |
| --- | --- | --- | --- | --- | --- | --- | --- | --- |
| | Narrow | Medium | Wide | Leg | Heel Flap | Heel to Toe | Toe | Total Foot Length |
| 6 | 7¼ | 8¼ | 9⅛ | 6½ | 2⅛ | 7⅝ | 1¾ | 9⅜ |
| 6½ | 7½ | 8⅜ | 9¼ | 6¾ | 2⅛ | 7¾ | 1⅞ | 9½ |
| 7 | 7⅝ | 8½ | 9⅜ | 6¾ | 2¼ | 7¾ | 2 | 9¾ |
| 7½ | 7¾ | 8¾ | 9½ | 6⅞ | 2¼ | 7¾ | 2 | 9¾ |
| 8 | 7⅞ | 8¾ | 9¾ | 7 | 2¼ | 8 | 2 | 10 |
| 8½ | 8⅛ | 9 | 9¾ | 7⅛ | 2¼ | 8¼ | 2 | 10¼ |
| 9 | 8¼ | 9⅛ | 10 | 7¼ | 2¼ | 8¼ | 2 | 10¼ |
| 9½ | 8⅜ | 9¼ | 10⅛ | 7⅜ | 2⅜ | 8½ | 2⅛ | 10⅝ |
| 10 | 8½ | 9⅜ | 10¼ | 7½ | 2⅜ | 8⅝ | 2⅛ | 10¾ |
| 10½ | 8¾ | 9½ | 10⅜ | 7⅝ | 2⅜ | 8¾ | 2⅛ | 10⅞ |
| 11 | 8¾ | 9¾ | 10⅝ | 7¾ | 2½ | 8⅞ | 2⅛ | 11 |
| 11½ | 9 | 9¾ | 10¾ | 7¾ | 2½ | 8⅞ | 2¼ | 11⅛ |
| 12 | 9⅛ | 10 | 10⅞ | 7⅞ | 2⅝ | 8⅞ | 2⅜ | 11¼ |
| 12½ | 9¼ | 10⅛ | 11 | 8⅛ | 2⅝ | 9⅛ | 2⅜ | 11½ |
| 13 | 9¾ | 10¼ | 11¼ | 8¼ | 2⅝ | 9¼ | 2⅜ | 11⅝ |
| 13½ | 9½ | 10⅜ | 11¼ | 8¼ | 2¾ | 9⅜ | 2⅜ | 11¾ |
| 14 | 9¾ | 10⅝ | 11½ | 8⅜ | 2¾ | 9⅝ | 2⅜ | 12 |
| 14½ | 9¾ | 10¾ | 11⅝ | 8⅝ | 2¾ | 9¾ | 2⅜ | 12⅛ |
| 15 | 10 | 10⅞ | 11¾ | 8¾ | 2¾ | 9⅞ | 2⅜ | 12¼ |

Foot Measurements and Shoe Sizes

# About the Authors

## Charlene Schurch

Charlene Schurch is the author of a growing number of knitting books and numerous magazine articles about knitting and spinning. Her articles have appeared in *Vogue Knitting, Knitters, Interweave Knits, Piecework,* and *SpinOff.* She divides her time between Connecticut and Florida.

## Beth Parrott

Although Beth Parrott has been knitting for more than 60 years, until recently she designed socks and other garments only for family and for charity projects. She loves to teach and is an avid collector of tricks-of-the-trade and tidbits of information that make knitting easier. She works, plays, knits, and teaches in Charleston, South Carolina.

---

**THERE'S MORE ONLINE**
To find more great knitting books,
visit www.martingale-pub.com.

# Index

KEY: **Bold** = chart; *italic* = photo